JOHNNY OWEN

Jeff Murphy was brought up in the small rural town of Kidwelly on the West Wales coast. He is a scriptwriter, author, musician and songwriter.

MAINSTREAM SPORT

JOHNNY OWEN

JEFF MURPHY

MAINSTREAM
PUBLISHING
EDINBURGH AND LONDON

**To the memory and fighting spirit
of Johnny Owen**

This edition, 2005

First published in Great Britain in 2004 by
MAINSTREAM PUBLISHING COMPANY (EDINBURGH) LTD
7 Albany Street
Edinburgh EH1 3UG

ISBN 1 84596 042 4

A catalogue record for this book is available from the British Library

Typeset in Alternate Gothic and Times
Printed and bound in Great Britain by
Cox & Wyman Ltd

ACKNOWLEDGEMENTS

Many thanks to Merthyr Tydfil Public Library and to every one of the kind and considerate library staff working there. Thanks for all their help and advice, including the use of rooms and equipment, and all the wonderfully kept files and folders containing thousands of articles and submissions relating to the whole of Johnny Owen's life and career.

Kind thanks to Christina Williams for all her help with early research in California, for US library visits, use of telephones and computers, calls to those involved in that last fight, and her emails chasing up all those concerned in the United Kingdom. Thanks to her for all the rides on the freeways to information, for the US/New York televised copy of the Owen versus Pintor fight and her exceptional early encouragement.

Thanks to all those at Salem Films and BBC Wales; Ynyr Williams, Dylan Richards and Huw Talfryn-Walters for all the background help, the experience of Mexico City and the success of the documentary.

A big thanks to Johnny's father, Dick Owens, for all his time, patience and energy, for all the wonderful chats and interviews in Merthyr Tydfil and Mexico City. For a real good week in Mexico, too, and for the use of some of his research documents and papers relating to Johnny Owen.

Thanks to Johnny's brother Kelvin Owens for sorting a few things out towards the end, and to Edith and Dick for all their hospitality, always at hand whenever I visited.

Thanks especially to Ken Bayliss, a Merthyr Tydfil writer, for a huge contribution in research and translation, for the discovery of articles relating to Johnny and for great moral support.

Special thanks to the unique Susan Kemp for keeping me going when I didn't want to do anything at all; for all the Internet searching, research input, for listening to my 'yabbering on' and for bringing me food.

Thanks to Michale Clemment, whose consistent support and constructive criticism mean a great deal. And to Mum and Dad for everything.

Special thanks to Harry Carpenter, surely the finest commentator on boxing ever. In one hour, one can learn so much.

Finally, to Gruff and Billy Hughes. Well played and rest now.

CONTENTS

Champions aren't made in gyms. Champions are made from something they have deep inside them — a desire, a dream, a vision. They have to have last-minute stamina, they have to be a little faster, they have to have the skill and the will. But the will must be stronger than the skill.

Muhammad Ali

INTRODUCTION

In September 1980, Ronald Reagan was campaigning for his first term of office as President of the United States of America. Margaret Thatcher's Government in the United Kingdom had begun to put into place policies that would eventually lead to the destruction of industry, challenge the power of the trades unions and ultimately change the face of British, European and, indeed, world politics for ever. A new Pope, John Paul II, after almost two years at the head of the world's most powerful Church, was easing his way into the job purposefully and meaningfully. Communism, through the collective will of the three new political forces about to be aligned and aimed fiercely against it, though it didn't know it at the time, was on its way out; its day done, the Cold War over. Technology was arriving in an unprecedented way and at an unprecedented speed and was almost on the street. Soon human beings would and could never be the same again. It was an axis point in world history. An important time for the old guard to make a last stand.

Johnny Owen, known as 'the Matchstick Man' because of his extraordinary skeletal physique, lived and died doing what he liked most, doing what he was meant to do, what he was born to do. Johnny

Owen died a young man, at the peak of his professional abilities, chasing his fondest dream, immersed in life and living, and loving every minute of it. *He lived and died beckoning a dream, doing what he loved the most.* How many of us left in his wake will arrive at the pearly gates with that motif inscribed as our earthly epitaph? How many of us honestly get to do what we really want in life? How many of us take to global, physical and philosophical limits our dreams and ambitions, and attempt to accomplish harmony within our lives by doing what we really love to do? Most of us never attain the heights that we perhaps ought to. To do what you really love, to set aside all things for dreams, is far too scary; far too risky a prospect for the vast majority of mortals, struggling to survive the icy blasts of a world society based on capital, to contemplate. A mixture of bad luck, geography, an unsteady footing, poor education, wrong turnings and a host of other natural social phenomena will account for the forgotten dreams of the rest of us. Best stay with bricks and mortar, and a career in social skills. Safer that way. Johnny Owen died boxing.

Those who still mourn Johnny Owen may never agree with the argument that this young, talented, gracefully skilful boxer might have been a lucky soul. That argument is powerful and just, however, and has a resonance with societies and traditions long gone. One day, just like Johnny, all of us will have an insight into the merits of that point of view. Our day, when it comes, will be an adventure into past reflections and glories. Did we fulfil our ambitions? Did we follow our dreams? Did we do what our hearts dictated we should? Johnny Owen did. He followed a true path in life, worked hard and never complained (or maybe rarely complained) and never wavered in the belief that one day, the dream would be his. He used his natural sporting talents and skills to organise his life to his advantage, and for his pleasure. Johnny Owen was, then, a successful man.

To all intents and purposes, the noble art of self-defence claimed Johnny's life on 19 September 1980 (although he heroically fought on in a deep coma as powerfully as he ever fought in a boxing ring for a further 46 days). He died far, far away from his beloved home town of Merthyr Tydfil. Far, far away from the land he loved so much and so closely identified with – Wales. He died in a very different place from home, in a hostile land governed and guided by very different principles and ideals from those he grew up with, from those that motivated and excited him. The United States of America could never be deemed a society that promoted the values of labour or social equality or close-knit community, at least not in the sense Johnny Owen understood them. The welcome the young man had received in the New World was not exactly a warm one either.

Los Angeles, at the heart of American culture, initially dismissed Johnny Owen's chances as a boxer. The media hounds and sceptical boxing analysts treated him badly, and made him feel inadequate and out of place. Some elements of the press ridiculed his physique and ability, and many refused to accept him as a worthy challenger. Johnny remained unfazed by all of this negative attention and slowly, ever so slowly, his detractors got to know him. And equally as slowly and deliberately, Johnny Owen began to win them over. At the end of this baptism of fire, this ritual courtship, they came to realise what the people of Wales knew all along about this extraordinary character, this wonderful charming man, this fighter with the courage of a lion and a heart of pure gold: that he was special. In the end, those who were at first critical embraced him completely. Such is the power of integrity, honesty and courage.

Johnny Owen's last powerful and courageous statement to the world was given to us from downtown Los Angeles in a fight that featured another hero in the rich history of the modern boxing arena: Guadalupe (Lupe) Pintor, the Mexican world bantamweight champion. The boxing match that would decide the bantamweight championship of the world was to take place in an area of Los Angeles that could best be described as 'Little Mexico'. Lupe Pintor, although defending his world title away from the country of his birth, might as well have been scrapping in his own backyard, for the support he was to receive from his fellow countrymen was massive, almost total. On top of that good fortune (as though he needed it), he was a tough, strong, arrogant, skilful, vicious champion, deemed by many 'impartial' observers and media 'experts' to be unbeatable. Johnny

Owen had almost been written off before he started. He certainly had his work cut out, there was no doubting that, and both he and his management and training team knew it. Lupe Pintor lay in wait for the man from the valleys of Wales – pantheresque, ready, confident, the odds stacked in his favour – seemingly only needing to turn up to retain his title. The Welshman would not – could not – underestimate such a foe.

This was a unique fight in many respects. A fight between the representatives of two countries bound by similarities of culture and history. The mighty USA towered above Mexico as the shadow of England hovered over all things Welsh. Post-industrial poverty and deprivation scarred both lands. Hunger for the possession of a better future drove both men. It was a fight between two great and proven boxers, both vying for their place in history, a fight between the champions of Europe and America, a fight of equals – although the American media had wrongly touted it as a walkover for Lupe Pintor. Johnny Owen, the great white Welsh hope, had come to Los Angeles for the crown. The great Mexican artist of the ring sought to hold that crown at all costs. This fight had possibilities. It had the promise of being a 'wonder fight'. Owen had the steel of the Welsh industrial valleys coursing through his veins and the stamina of an Ethiopian long-distance runner in reserve to fall back on at all times. Pintor had a repertoire full of the finest skills a boxer could possess. He also had a hell of a punch. Something Johnny Owen was lacking in his armoury.

As it turned out, and against all the odds, the young, seemingly malnourished Welsh boxer, the Matchstick Man from Merthyr Tydfil, almost took away the spoils and returned them and the crown of world champion to the industrial valley of his birth. Almost . . .

Young men go into the brutal and self-destructive activity of boxing for a host of assorted motivations. Some of them verge on the bitterly antisocial. Some are psychotic. Some have been forced to better themselves to escape, while others are very often angry, from socially inadequate backgrounds. Some just love boxing. Johnny Owen came from Merthyr Tydfil at the end of the industrial age, a town where unemployment and poverty were rife. Johnny loved boxing, but he would have been very aware of his social status too. Aware and perhaps a little angry.

There must be an anger that initially drives the boxer. It is the landscape from which he has sprung that helps him unaided into the ring for the first time and the subtext that keeps him there when all else seems lost and utterly hopeless. And if boxers are angry, one would have to be stupidly naive not to know why, negligent and blasé not to see the reasons. For the most part, boxers constitute the disenfranchised in our wealthy, commerce-driven society. They are the sons of the ghettos, the old industrial towns, the countries without riches or opportunity, where anger, if not crazed fury, is a more appropriate course of behaviour against the system that has them in chains than the rational, liberal debate of their more fortunate peers. There are no world boxing champions educated at Eton. Prince Charles's boys are not leaping in for a ten-rounder with the holder of any boxing championship in their vicinity. Both Johnny Owen and Lupe Pintor hailed from societies one could deem 'tough and industrial', with hardship a daily, normal experience. Both may well have been angry once. But in almost every case of boxers that set out on the road to glory, to fight their way out, the anger is soon replaced. It soon disappears.

After all, there is so much self-discipline involved, so much craft to be learned, so much else to take on board beside one's original motives for fighting, that anger and bitterness become clouded, vague, and very often completely lost and forgotten. Many good, experienced fighters become kind and gentle people. They leave their fight in the ring. And even in the ring, they rarely get angry. It is an expensive stimulant. It uses up energy at an alarming rate. It is impractical to get mad. The boxer is trained to fight until he cannot go on, trained not to burn out before his chance to win, his chance to dispose of the challenge, finally arrives for him. No sport is more physical or direct than boxing. No sport more brutal, more artistic or hypnotically beautiful than boxing. And when the match is set up correctly, no sport is more exciting.

A boxing match is a story, one in which anything can happen. In the pages that follow, the story of that fight – the night and the boxing match, the World Championship bout between Lupe Pintor and Johnny Owen in Los Angeles, the 'Battle of Little Mexico' – will unfold. But the story of how Johnny Owen almost realised his dream to become world bantamweight champion is not the only tale to tell, important though it is. That challenge to Lupe Pintor's superiority is part of a bigger and more universal tale. There is also the story of the aftermath of that night in 1980. The long goodbye and the fallout that will always be there. The 'what happened next' story: poignant, emotional and surprisingly uplifting. Finally, there's the real, heart-warming story of how Johnny Owen got to that place at that time. How he got from relative obscurity to be a world 'contender' in such a short space of time. How the dream unfolded for the kid from Merthyr Tydfil.

In the course of researching for this book, I have been made acutely aware of the three separate stages of the story involved in the short life of Johnny Owen. Three journeys to examine, each equally as important as the others. One of which I became physically and, to a certain extent, fundamentally a part of. And each piece of the story – the beginning, middle and end – must be in place to ensure that the big picture adds up. The past, the present and the future together bind the Johnny Owen story. There is an old North American Indian saying: *'Your past is a skeleton walking one step behind you. Your future is a skeleton walking one step in front of you. Maybe you don't wear a watch, but your skeletons do. They always know what time it is. The time is now. And you and I are trapped there.'*

Past, present and future determine, for each and every one of us, who we are. If we are wise, we understand that the elements that will allow us freedom and the rein we need to move forward with confidence and hope are there for us all. We can all go for the dream if we want.

In the spring of 2002, it was time for my journey to begin. In the context of this book, it is the first of three journeys. In the present, we were to revisit the past and, through that visit to days gone by, determine the future for those so closely involved. My 'I was there' trip, as the internationally acclaimed Welsh entertainer Max Boyce might say, began in March of that year. I had been involved in the development, production, research and writing of the BBC Wales/Salem Films BAFTA award-winning (as it turned out) documentary film, *Johnny Owen: The Long Journey*. The film firmly centred its theme on life after Johnny Owen, establishing as its central and main character Dick Owens, the boxer's ageing father. As assistant to the producer, I was to travel with Dick Owens and the rest of the team on an eight-day film shoot to Mexico City. We were heading there to meet an old adversary of Dick's, and it was there that I was honoured to receive a unique insight into the world of boxing and listen to many of Dick Owens' reminiscences. I spent most of my downtime on that warm Mexican week taking notes for this book and chatting with Johnny's sharp-as-ever ex-trainer.

The filmmakers followed Dick around the vast metropolis that is Mexico City as he searched for and found, then finally met and confronted the man who had both finished his career as a boxing trainer and ended his son's short life – Lupe Pintor. The two men had not seen each other since that awful, fateful night in Los Angeles in September 1980.

Dick's successful pilgrimage ended many years of anguish for both men. It was a time for resolution and, in the space of a few short minutes after meeting, they were clearly at ease. This had been what both of them had so desperately needed. After an initial time of quiet and dignified 'getting to know each other', the two older and now wiser fighting pros settled down to talk boxing. Before long, they had become friends. Through retrospective understanding of what had taken place all those years ago, they reflected on the past and cast aside any bad feeling, imagined or otherwise, and made a new beginning. Lupe Pintor, truly a giant among boxing 'greats', cried tears of relief as Dick uttered words of forgiveness. Dick Owens cried tears of joy as he hugged the younger man, who clearly needed his compassion and mercy as much as Dick needed some kind of closure with the Mexican former bantamweight world boxing champion.

For those of us who stood on the sidelines that day, this was a truly moving experience. And when it was over, a drink or two (a drink or two too many for some) was gladly taken. For the remainder of the week, Dick and I continued discussing the life and profession of Johnny Owen, complaining about the overwhelming Mexican traffic, the terribly spicy food and the difficulties of finding our way around downtown Mexico City. We talked solidly about Johnny Owen and Lupe Pintor and Mexico and Los Angeles and Merthyr Tydfil and fighters and all sorts. We talked the week away.

When I arrived back home in Wales, I began to study another journey: the rise of Johnny Owen, the boxer. His climb from childhood protégé, roaming the backstreets of his home town looking for a boxing match, to a real and genuine World Championship contender. This was the journey which carved out the path that took the young man to his last fight. This was the journey to the stars, the journey of hope, the journey that would bring back the world title to Merthyr Tydfil and Wales. It would be Johnny Owen's most famous journey. At its conclusion lay the flight to the United States and the rainbow's end.

Johnny Owen, his dad and trainer Dick Owens, and the magnificent Dai Gardner, surely one of the United Kingdom's best-ever managers of boxers, embarked upon this adventure more or less alone. What happened in the time they spent together in pursuit of their dream has been wonderfully well documented in journals, periodicals and newspapers, and in the memories of those who were there. Through all of this, and through many first-hand experiences, a glimpse of the reality of what a tilt at the world title really means was afforded to me.

The third and final journey deals with the character of the man: Johnny Owen, the person. Who was he? What made him tick? Why did the world's watching sporting aficionados, boxing fans and non-boxing fans empathise so closely with him? Why did he love the sport of boxing above all else? How did he become so popular so quickly? Why did his life-and-death struggle feature so loudly in the world's media? And what was it about Johnny Owen's passing that made us all weep so? The trip from extremely humble beginnings to being almost the bantamweight champion of the world was long and sometimes complex. Johnny Owen travelled it in confident style.

Johnny Owen died because he took part in a boxing match. Questions about the legitimacy of the sport would seem to surface because of this one unassailable fact. There are those who say that boxing should be abolished; they say that boxing is the only sport in which the objective is to cause injury, where the brain is the target and knockout is the goal. Campaigns are frequently launched to ban it altogether. If they were to succeed, then boxing would simply be driven underground. The arguments for and against the legality of boxing are legion. They will not be resurrected here. This is the story of Johnny Owen. It is not a biography or an intellectual bargaining chip for either of the 'for' or 'against' camps that seek boxing as their own. It is the story of a boxer who epitomised every boxer that has ever lived. From his background to his rise to fame, he is archetypal of the professional in the world of professional boxing.

Johnny Owen was a wonderful boxer. Perhaps the best Wales has ever known. He'd be the first to deny that, perhaps in favour of his beloved Jimmy Wilde, the 'Ghost with a Hammer in his Hand', but his record stands up to intense scrutiny in much the same way as any of the Welsh boxing legends' records do. Tommy Farr, Eddie Thomas, Howard Winstone, Jimmy Wilde and Johnny Owen are among the best that have ever emerged from the Welsh Valleys. All will figure prominently – or not so prominently, as the case may be – in the pages that follow, as they feature in and influence Johnny Owen's boxing life.

There are many good arguments as to who was the greatest Welsh boxer of all. Those arguments continue on and on as boxing continues on and on. The sport is as strong now in the twenty-first century as it ever was in the twentieth, though it has changed somewhat in style, substance and presentation. And even if Johnny Owen was not the greatest of all the Welsh fighters, not the greatest of all the bantamweights that have ever fought, one has to doubt whether there has ever been a more affable, phlegmatic, charming, well-liked fighter anywhere and at any time.

This book represents what I feel is the 'story' of Johnny Owen. It is not an official biography of the great boxer nor is it an academic, sociological or psychological study that will attempt to unravel the secrets of boxing or challenge the sport's validity. I don't claim to be a boxing expert either. It is my story. A dedication, if you like, to a superb and heroic contemporary whose kind we may never see in the world of sports, or indeed in any other arena in modern society, ever again. It is also the story of a journey to Mexico City and details many of the events that took place there in March 2002. Much that follows derives from what happened and what was learned during that journey to Mexico. A lot more of the detail was to come from interviews and correspondence with those who remember and have survived the passing of the years. The rest was researched at Merthyr Tydfil Public Library, and other reference libraries in the UK and beyond.

For me, Johnny Owen is one of the great sporting heroes of my lifetime. He was someone who reflected the change that was blowing through the valleys and mining towns of old Wales at the start of the 1980s, a crucial time. He represented a decency and dignity that sportsmen and women are supposed to carry with them as examples to the young hero-worshippers that follow their every move. He represented a courage we should all aspire to. His dedication and application are an example to everyone. He was a wonderful ambassador for boxing. And he is still held in huge regard long after his death.

The greatest boxing commentator of them all, Harry Carpenter, said to me over a recent luncheon meeting that Johnny Owen had been one of the most well-mannered, affable and deferential of characters he had ever had the pleasure of interviewing. High praise, indeed. And this 20-odd years on!

Johnny Owen was magic. Ask those who worked with him, those who knew him. Something separates champions from the rest of us. Johnny was a champion – European, United Kingdom, Commonwealth, in every walk of life and in the way he dealt with those around him. Johnny was a true man of courage and he deserves his place in both the history of boxing and the history of Wales. He was a man of great dignity and a credit to his sport, and, although never a world champion, he deserves all the accolades accorded to that class of boxer regardless. In a quiet moment in Mexico City, I asked Lupe Pintor, through an interpreter, what he thought of Johnny, the fighter. He shook his head and whistled through his teeth. He needn't have gone on.

1

MEXICO BOUND

Saint Peter went in to speak to God. Looking down on Wales, he said: 'Lord, why have you been so generous to the Welsh? They have beautiful mountains, fine lakes, magnificent beaches. What have these people done to earn all these treasures?'

'All these treasures?' replied the Lord. 'Have you seen who I've given them as neighbours?'

Traditional Welsh satire

It was a dark, dreary, early March, end-of-winter-type morning. I felt as though I'd had little or no sleep. It was difficult to quite remember in the dull haze of middle-of-the-night blues, but I was pretty sure I'd had none. The pre-travel hype and excitement for the journey ahead, and a brain full of the normal concerns as to whether or not all arrangements had been tended to and would work to plan had certainly taken their toll as I lay there tossing and turning in anxious, dream-deprived turmoil. Sleep does not come easy on nights such as these. Add to that the fact that I was subconsciously aware that I had to be up and about and alert and active by 2 a.m., and the possibilities for any kind of decent slumber diminished considerably. The odds must have been 33–1 at least for any pukka kip ensuing.

Anyway, a car had been ordered for me. That much I knew.

Courtesy of the production company responsible for the making of our little documentary film. My own airport taxi. How marvellous to not be standing at a cold, unsheltered, weather-beaten train station, or tossed around on the splendid high roads of England and Wales in an non-air-conditioned 1970s super-luxury coach. My car duly arrived at 2.30 a.m., on the proverbial dot, and it whisked me off showered, dressed and shaved to Cardiff's International Airport. There, I would catch the shuttle flight to Amsterdam and, in the very Dutch and sterile concourse that is Schiphol, would further await the main journey across the Atlantic on a much uglier and more gruesome jumbo jet (how do those things stay up?) to Mexico City.

At about the same socially unacceptable time as I was making my way, a man much older and wiser than I, the ex-boxing trainer and father of the subject of our documentary was leaving an equally drab and dreary, early-morning Merthyr Tydfil deep in the heart of industrial Wales. Dick Owens was much closer to Cardiff, but his journey to the airport would be a less scenic trip than mine. My journey from Carmarthen in the west of Wales offered the promise of countryside. Dick would have travelled from the bleak ex-coal-and-steel town along a more industrial route. Not that it mattered too much, I suppose, in the bleary-eyed dank darkness that greeted us both. The journey ahead for Dick Owens that morning would also be more tiring, stressful and anxious than mine could ever be. It was to be, at least in its planning, a far more intense and thoughtful time for him.

My taxi driver talked and talked and talked all the way up the M4, the motorway that leads from South Wales to London (I would leave it at Cardiff). He didn't appear to stop. He may have, but I don't recall it. It was all I needed, the icing on the early-morning cake. Here was someone uplifting and happy when I needed misery and silence to accompany my sombre mood. I wondered what he'd been taking to keep himself awake, but soon realised, catching one or two of his finer points, that for him the nightshift was almost ending. He was hyped up for home. After me, it was over. I supposed that it also came as a blessed relief to be transporting someone not in an alcoholic stupor to a destination that didn't involve the chasing of more booze or badly cooked meat. For him, the night was ending well. The revellers would be more or less off the streets by the time he clocked off. I allowed the journey to lapse into silence for a while, sealing out my travelling companion's parables with a daydream (if you can have daydreams at 3 a.m.). I stared out through a window still spotted with old rain and with just a hint of condensation layering its surface. All along the M4 corridor, away from the nightclubs and late-night, early-morning drinkers, the world seemed soundly asleep. It was a time for poets and thinkers, a time for good conversation, a time for the universe to assert its power over all things mortal, a time to reflect. A time to travel to airports.

St David's Day – 1 March – had been and gone. The patron saint of Wales had had his day on a Friday that year, just two days earlier, and missed the annual early-March rugby international between Wales and Italy at Cardiff's 'wonder of the world' Millennium Stadium by one day. Many of the principality's workforce had taken off the long weekend to accommodate both the patron saint and the rugby team. Reasons for skiving off were both wonderful and legion. Anyone with half a brain could list them at will. After all, didn't they have the country's national pride and interest at heart? Weren't they supporting the real political cause of the day and socking it to the European Union and the English? Excuses could be given to all that required them on a shaky Monday morning (or Tuesday, depending on the alcohol intake) accompanied by the flag of Wales – the red dragon – a gargantuan hangover and the good news that the team had won. That would certainly help any cause – winning always does – and allow almost any excuse to be believed.

Many moons ago, the Welsh rugby team had been world class. Now, they struggled. Struggled to define their purpose and place in this new era of rugby professionalism, struggled to structure the new sport, struggled with its ruthlessness and commercially driven concepts. But now they had a new coach. Having lost the last one to New Zealand. The future looked good. This one was a Kiwi too and he had done well in his inaugural outing against the relatively new boys of the now Six Nations Championship, tournament outsiders

Italy. Wales recorded the first win of this 'new era' with the score 44–20. Steve Hansen was the new boy and his team had won comfortably but unconvincingly. A victory was a victory nonetheless. These days, in this new world of over-competitive international rugby, any win for Wales would be received joyously and grabbed with open arms. Hansen's side played well for 20 minutes of each half, but never gained the overall control they had threatened. It was a good start, but not a great one. This would give our travelling group something to chat about while we waited for the KLM shuttle to Amsterdam airport. I would bring it up in order to break the ice and get us all yapping. It had certainly occupied my taxi driver's thoughts over the last few miles. He was very pleased with the turn of events that had the Welsh team winning. I let him go on (and on) and just listened. I'd missed the match, so I needed the information.

Rugby and boxing always make for good conversation in Wales, but mostly rugby. And the conversation is always enhanced mightily in defeat. There's nothing like sorting out the national team's problems and getting to the nitty gritty of Welsh politics through rugby. A win allows for less criticism. It's not so much fun in the fallout. What can be more boring than an easy win? Who would there be to pick on? What players can the barflies and would-be selectors banish to the Australian outback and beyond, maybe even to rugby league, for being useless, hopeless, hapless, clueless and out of touch? Winning is great, but for a good old-fashioned discussion, losing is better.

I was the first to arrive at Cardiff airport. I bade farewell to my hyperactive, end-of-shift driver and approached a near-empty airport terminal (near-empty except for those on charter flights to assured sunshine and Malaga, that is) with a little apprehension and some nervousness. This was not a cakewalk of a trip by any means. There was no 'gimme' here. We had no idea how things would work out. Mexico City would be different for sure and Lupe Pintor, the ex-bantamweight champion of the world and conqueror of our hero Johnny Owen, an unknown quantity. He lay in wait at our destination as the second principal character in the story. Banishing all negative thoughts, I found a quiet area to wait and sat down for a good ponder about the possibilities the week ahead might have in store. Very soon, the notebook was out.

Dick Owens was the next to arrive. At first, seemingly bright and buoyant, and up for the trip. Dick was a big man, but not overly so. He looked in special health and, for someone who was 75 years old, he was full of life. Here was a young man in an older man's physical presence. But he, like me, had not been troubled too greatly by sleep that night. My first impression of buoyancy soon gave way to a second, of drowsiness. Yawning gives much away. Some say it is a sign of nervousness, and I'd agree, but on this occasion, I'd say that the yawning was simply a sign of us being plain tired. We shook hands, said our hellos and agreed sleep could wait for us both till we boarded the main 13-hour flight out from Amsterdam to Mexico. I closed my notebook and we sat together in the terminal. Almost immediately, we got stuck into the travel arrangements like old pros, quickly denigrating those who had organised this trip, in the middle of the night, with two planes to Mexico and not one, as 'amateurs'.

'We should have arranged it all. It would have been so much better. What the bloody hell are we doing here at 3.30 in the morning? It's all right for those over there going to Malaga,' we pointed. 'They're off on holiday to the sunshine!' On and on we droned. We pretended it was work and we were not really there to enjoy the experience. But we were. And we kept complaining. It was a good feeling at that time of the day to have a decent target to aim at. Someone to whinge about! Someone not around to defend himself. It broke the ice and calmed the nerves. We didn't mean it, of course. This was just the done thing. One always has to have a go at the travel arrangements first. Soon, in Mexico City, we would moan about the hotel.

The documentary's director was next through the terminal doors. Dylan Richards is a young, relaxed, no-nonsense professional with a feel for the great project and a very ambitious eye on the future. Both Dick and I had met him briefly once, maybe twice, before. He seemed to understand instinctively what was needed at all times. Quiet and reserved, he kept his own counsel. It was easy to assume through the periods of thoughtful silence that he was debating and deciding upon the fate of the film. He could just as easily have been wondering how his William Hill betting account had got into such a mess, for all I knew. He gave little away. Dylan remained quiet and reserved all the way to Mexico City.

With all three of us now present, and the film's producer and cameraman already heading for Mexico via another assignment in New York, we decided to check in and head off for a cup of tea. We still had quite a time to wait out before the flight to Amsterdam, still a long way to go, but it was reasonable to assume that the time would pass pleasantly and quickly enough. The surroundings were fine, the company interesting. As I predicted it would, the conversation soon came around to rugby union and the national team. Little was said about the real reason for our journey. There was no need to go there; we all knew what we were about. So, we kept Mexico and Johnny Owen and Lupe Pintor in the subtext at all times. Soon, the announcer blasted out that KLM Flight 102 to Amsterdam was ready for boarding. We were on our way. The shuttle flight over to the Dutch mainland was quick and efficient, and enjoyable. We shared the aircraft with many of the defeated Italian national rugby team returning home, tail between legs, a beaten force. It was a good day to be travelling.

The wait in Schiphol Airport was long. We managed to find some good-looking armchairs and some decent food, and Dick and I got talking about boxing and Johnny Owen. He was looking forward to meeting Lupe Pintor, looking forward to Mexico City, but with some trepidation. I was interested in finding out everything I could about boxing itself. I'd never met a real boxer let alone a world champion, although my grandfather had trained a boxer or two in his time, which was before I was around, I might add. As with all things, when two Welshmen from the industrial homeland get talking, politics is never too far away from the surface. It inhabits and inhibits the train of thought as though bred to do so. Dick's answers to many of my questions were often fused with belief and delivered in layered explanation.

I asked him about boxing and his life as a trainer. He talked about young boxers and Johnny Owen as a young man. He talked about his career as a trainer and how, time and again, boxing in the tough Merthyr Tydfil valley turned out better human beings. It rarely failed. He believed boxing to be a bit like national service in its outcome. The training and the acceptance are hard work, but when you get there, when it's all finished and done, you are a man, you know your power and you are able to control it. Very often this becomes the key to every success in life, the understanding of what you are and who you are, and where you fit in. Dick talked around Johnny. Spoke a lot about his training days and remembered fondly the thrill of having a new boxer start in the gym – young, full of hopes and dreams, not knowing his right hand from his left, not being able to skip or exercise or box. He discussed how the discipline needed to become a boxer took hold, how the young man became more and more proficient in his craft. Rightly or wrongly, he believed that boxing made real men and good citizens out of young and very often tearaway youths. It kept them off the streets, built into them great self-esteem and taught them respect for others, for those around them, and for those who knew a little about life. Boxing taught them to listen, to feel things, to be aware at all times.

Anyone who knows anything about boxing will tell you that it's a tough old sport. To get to the top, a person has to be special. He must be 100 per cent dedicated, 100 per cent committed, 100 per cent in tune with what is needed. That's to get to the top. To become a champion, or a challenger to the champion, one has to have something extra as well as all the dedication, commitment and insight. To be in the champions' league, one has to have something indefinable. Something inside that is extra to everything else. Dick only worked with one such champion during his time as a trainer and that fighter was his son Johnny Owen. He was different. Throughout his career and in every fight, Johnny gave everything he had, and was tactically and mentally aware at all times during a bout. He trained hard, worked hard, and maintained his diet and weight throughout his professional career without ever complaining. Boxers like Johnny Owen are rare and are every trainer's dream.

We talked of lots more. It wasn't always boxing and not always about Johnny. After a quick cuppa, a call home and a wake-up wash to freshen up, the long hours of waiting vanished and it was time to fly away to Mexico City. At long last.

I stood behind Dick Owens in the long line for boarding. I stood chatting away to Dylan Richards about nothing much really other than the queuing and waiting associated with travel, and how tedious it all was and of the weather differential we'd notice when we got to Mexico. Then it occurred to me, as I guess it must have occurred to Dylan, that there would have been so much going through Dick Owens' mind at this stage. So many old memories were about to be resurrected for him. So much of the old way and the old life would be rummaged through in the week ahead.

Dick had not trained or been involved in boxing since his retirement from the ring in 1980. He had been asked to go to Mexico City to meet Lupe Pintor by the production team organising the documentary we were about to film. He was apprehensive. Especially about meeting Lupe Pintor. He had not seen or spoken to Pintor since the Mexican world champion fought Johnny Owen on 19 September 1980.

Dick would also be required to attend a night out at a boxing bill in Mexico City. He hadn't been near a boxing ring since that night in 1980 either. Further, it could be presumed that there would be one or two other surprises in store for him along the way. It would be a tiring and emotionally draining week for him. Lupe Pintor was still associated with boxing. We were aware of that. He was doing Dick's old job, training youngsters to box, so we'd heard. That would be another odd realisation to contend with. It was little wonder the man from Merthyr Tydfil was a mite nervous.

On the flight out from Amsterdam to Mexico, Dick and I sat together. Drinks were brought to relax us and pretty decent food served to settle us down. I enjoy flying. It is something I have no problem with. Dick seemed relaxed, too. We talked for a while longer about Johnny Owen, boxing, the trip ahead, about Merthyr Tydfil and

Mexico, and for both of us fatigue gradually overcame consciousness. It was time to sleep. Time to try and get rid of some of this journey to a land neither of us had ever seen before. I wondered what my fellow traveller was thinking. What dreams would he dream? Was this flight to meet Lupe Pintor reminiscent of the flight 22 years earlier that took him and his young son Johnny Owen to Los Angeles, and on to that fateful boxing match? Who could know? What one did know, or could more or less accurately guess was this – that the last fight between Johnny Owen and Lupe Pintor would be replayed time and again during the week to come through conversations, in interviews and in quiet reflection. I hoped it would be OK. I hoped everything would work out well. I hoped that it would not be too much for Johnny's old trainer and best friend to deal with. I noticed Dylan Richards already asleep in the seat opposite ours. The plane droned on and on. Dick had also succumbed to some shut-eye. Gradually, one gets used to the incessant, monotonous engine noise and eventually forgets about it. Slowly and without artificial assistance, much-needed sleep arrived for me too.

We could all dream now.

2

GLADIATORS (1)

Men fighting one another with only their fists and their cunning
are all contemporaries, all brothers, and like the crowd they play
to, they belong to no historical time.

Joyce Carol Oates, *On Boxing*

He was ahead. He was certain of that. After all, hadn't he won most of
the earlier rounds? Sure, the Mexican was on top of the fight now.
Especially in rounds nine and ten, and here in round eleven. But he
was still hopeful. The title was his. He could feel it. And he would
never give up. Never! Not while there was still hope.

He knew Lupe Pintor always did his best work at the end of his
fights. Hell, he'd known that for months. That was the whole point in
going after him in the first five rounds. So now he reckoned that if he
stood up against the final expected barrage, then there had to be hope.
He could win. Think positively, Johnny. Keep him at bay. Stay alert.
Move and move and move, and keep moving, and the judges would
still, just still, give it to him. If there was no hope what was the point?
Might as well have stayed at home.

He'd been hurt as early as the fifth round, hurt and cut, hurt and hit,
and was hurting big-time now. But Pintor was hurt, too. He'd picked
up on it. He knew it for sure. You sense pain in your opponent. You
sense trouble. And Pintor was troubled. But now, though, the huge cut

inside his mouth bothered him more than anything else did, even more than Pintor's body punches, suddenly all on target, for the first time, an added worry. His kidneys were raw. His ribs were aching. His vision was blurred. But the cut was the baddie here. What day is it? The gash inside the mouth wouldn't go away. It had weakened him badly. Psychologically bugged him. It had been with him for the last six rounds and the blood had poured through the gaping hole. He'd swallowed the lot.

Here comes Lupe Pintor. World bantamweight champion. Circling the ring. Stalking. Hunting. Haunting. Chasing. Sizing him up. Preparing his attack. Weighing the odds. Moving in. Master of the sweet science of bruising. Ready to strike. Striking NOW! Move, Johnny! Move! The crowd roars. It's deafening, frightening, all inspired by the Mexican champion. This is their champion. Their king! There's nowhere to hide. Nowhere to hide. The referee, like some distant Holy Ghost, says something. He can hardly hear him, but nods yes he's OK. But he needs the bell. Where's the bell? Where's the bell when you need it? Please, ring the bell. Bring on the bell. It's the only sound he wants hear. The only sound he will hear and welcome now.

Lupe Pintor throws a left. It misses. He smells the glove and yearns for the dressing-room and the comfort of the wintergreen, and the hot, sweet tea that Dick always has ready waiting for him. A body shot comes in under his heart. He hits back. His arm melts before him. No strength left. Lupe Pintor is quickly out of range. Gone like a ghost. Can't catch him. Heavy legs, legs heavy. Got to keep moving.

He's running on empty. It's the last chance saloon and there are no new ideas. Pintor at 5 ft 4 in. had been shorter than expected. He'd had a good height advantage. That had been pleasing. But had he used it properly? Yes! He had cut off the ring, stopped him being fancy. Used his reach, his craft and his courage. But had it worked? The bell! Thank God. Towel, stool, water, spit, blood, sweat and tears, bedlam and time to pause for thought. 'Be proud!' is the shout. And so he should.

He could rightly be proud. Hadn't he shown them? All that ridicule, the no-hoper stuff, the press at home and abroad saying he shouldn't be there, that he was out of his depth, out of his class. What the hell did they know? It was their arrogance that drove him on now. Their ignorance that made him stay when maybe he should have quit. Yes, he was here to win the title, to fight for Wales and all those he loved, and all the rest of it, but there was more to this, much, much more. This had become personal and he had something to prove.

They had ridiculed his very being. The way he looked, his manner and demeanour, his sticky-out ears, his unique and extremely vulnerable (or so they thought) skeletal frame, even his brightness. So what if he talked slowly and seemed at times to be behind the eight-ball for brains? He wasn't here to win *Mastermind*. This wasn't a beauty contest.

He was Welsh to the bone and to the centre of his soul! He was from Merthyr Tydfil and proud of it. He came into the ring draped in the Welsh flag. The Welsh Dragon! Most of the audience hadn't an earthly clue as to what the thing was. 'Wales, England?' they said. 'You from Wales, England, buddy?'

'No fear, mate. I'm from Wales, Wales. Ever heard of it?' A couple of guys thought that Wales was in Scotland! One of them pointed to Cornwall and one journalist stuck it in France, for Christ sakes! And, all the time, they criticised him, ridiculed him, played down his chances and made him feel small and made his corner team feel smaller. 'Amateurs' some had called them. Nothing hurts more than that.

He was no amateur. Welsh champion, British champion, Commonwealth champion, European champion – there was nothing amateur about that! What more could they want? Trouble was, if it hadn't happened on the other side of the Atlantic, it hadn't happened at all. He was here by rights. The best there was in the whole of Europe and beyond. They had the cheek to call it a mismatch in some circles of the press out there! That was deeply insulting to titles he had won. To call it a mismatch would be to devalue the crowns he wore. Forget it!

He and Dick had worked hard to get there. Dick was his personal trainer and the best father a boy could have. He was a mixture of heart and steel, of integrity and cunning and guile. Streetwise and honest, Dick had guile in spades and he had taught Johnny everything he knew. Taught him well. Each day, they'd be together. He kept Johnny running near their Merthyr home from Talybont reservoir to the top of the Gellideg housing estate, across the Brecon Beacons, three days a week, then along the seven miles from Cefn Vaynor to Swansea Road on the other three. In the afternoons, Johnny would chop down pine trees and spend the evenings sparring, but throwing no punches. He'd become master of the jump rope, thanks to Dick, and could effortlessly spin the rope over his head. Watching ropework very often hypnotised his audience. And now he was fitter than anyone he knew and as tough as old boots. That alone had shocked and surprised the Mexican. Next to Dick that night stood Dai Gardner.

Dai had been there almost from the start. At least since he'd been a pro. Dai's heart was in the right place but sometimes his head was out of sync. Hell, he was a manager. There's a whole different point of view when money is on the table. It makes you look at life in a different way sometimes. Dai always had Johnny's future at heart, though. Managers can get misunderstood. If Dai didn't think of the money, then who would? Money! If you want misunderstanding bring in money. Hadn't Dai got this Championship bid for him? Wheeling, dealing, talking to the press, keeping all the distractions away, organising the travel, hotels, interviews. He had set it all up. And look at the place! The Olympic Stadium, Los Angeles! Packed to the rafters. Mexicans baying for blood, Johnny's blood! And the critics eating their words because here he was, about to go out for the 12th and final round, and still in the fight.

The Mexican supporters didn't bother him either. They were mainly downtrodden, badly paid illegal immigrants just screaming for their man. He understood and forgave. All he wanted was the title. This contest was what his whole life had been about. If the fight had been in Wales, what then? These Mexicans were loving every single minute of it. No one supports boxing like a Mexican. For every champion, there are a hundred or so wannabes waiting in the wings in downtown

Mexico City. They breed champion boxers like the Welsh once bred outside-halves in rugby. To be a champ in Mexico was special. You had to be good, very good. His wonderful opponent, Lupe Pintor, had earned all this huge support and, over the years, the respect of his Welsh counterpart and challenger. He was a great champion: a natural, a real fighter and he'd worked for everything he had.

To beat Lupe would be special and not easy, and against all the predictions of all the experts and pundits and critics, and maybe even against the judgement of those closest to him. Johnny knew this. Johnny knew that he'd have to box out of his skin to win, to prove them all wrong. Johnny knew he would likely lose if he weren't at his best. He had to be at his very best. He'd go down badly if he was not at his best. He knew that. But he wouldn't lose without a real fight, a titanic struggle. He wouldn't let go without letting Lupe Pintor know he'd been in a fight. Johnny Owen, 'the Pride of Merthyr' they called him, and yes, he could stand proud. But now he had to stand again for the 12th round.

He could hardly stand at all when he came back to his stool, to buy time to breathe, rejuvenate, time to think. First, he thought of lies. A boxer must lie to be any good – a feint, a left-hook off the jab, an opening, thinking one thing, doing another – it's all lies. And he would have to find some good lies to survive the next round, to survive this fight. He knew that. Then he thought, 'motivation!' Motivation was what he needed, not from the outside but from the inside. He had to motivate himself. So, he thought of Ali and Frazier, the 'Thriller in Manila', then again of Ali. The courage of Ali was the template for all in the modern boxing era. That courage to go where no one had gone before. To find inner strength where you thought emptiness lay. That's what he had to do, find that inner strength. Would the greats of the ring give in just because of fatigue? No, they damn well wouldn't! So, when Dick asked if he wanted to go back in for the 12th, he was bound to say yes. 'We haven't come here to throw in the towel, Dad!' he thought to himself. And the bell sounded. And it was time to fight again.

Boxing is a dramatic art, on a par with anything the dramatists of the ballet, theatre and Hollywood could possibly come up with. Every fight tells a unique story. There is no script. Each participant has to have grace, agility, razor-sharp reflexes, split-second reaction times, the eyes of a tiger, the heart of a lion, fast hands, dancing feet, a body tuned to peak fitness and stamina. And then more stamina, and when all the stamina has run out, more courage.

The ring is 18 feet square. There is no escape.

And when all the boxer's assets have been used up and there is nothing left, and they are at the bottom of that dark well where only hope survives, more courage must be drawn from somewhere yet again. The result of any match, at World Championship level, hangs on the slightest of percentage differences in skills between two champions, and minute fractions in ability separate victory and defeat. Johnny was truly weary. The crowd bayed for Lupe Pintor to end the fight, to go for the kill. Suddenly, the Welsh, in a minority of 100–1 at least in this vast crowd, had stopped singing. The silence was eerie. It is a silence that comes in defeat. When the supporters of the hero know. They know and sense en masse that they are to lose. And they know a long, long time before the result comes. Once that psyche has established itself as the norm with those supporting, it transfers to the competitor. All is lost from that point on. Lupe Pintor had got the second wind he had hoped for. It had, luckily for him, amazingly surfaced from somewhere, somewhere deep within. And it made him dangerous.

The Mexicans in the crowd surged. Their man was going to win. They knew it. Johnny wasn't seeing a lot of the punches now. He jerks back a fraction from being hit. Lupe Pintor circles him in a movement that is off balance, but soon becomes a dance. Another jab misses him. Just. Everything seems to be happening at great speed and yet in slow motion. It's hard to explain. It's as though one's life was being re-run, and still one has to deal with the present. But when the punch landed it changed everything.

In one fraction of a second, the whole world turned upside down. And it wasn't Johnny's world that flipped. He was all right now. He was sleeping. Dreaming, oblivious to it all. No, the change came for those around him. For those around him, life would never, ever be the same again. In one nanosecond of power, ferocity and strength of self-preservation, Lupe Pintor had not only destroyed a dream, he had laid to rest a unique Welsh legend.

When the punch landed and the fighter was knocked out, onto the ground, the boxing ambitions of the great and courageous Johnny Owen, and of all those wonderful Welsh who supported him, and the town from which he sprang and the dreams of fortune and holidays abroad and hotels by the sea, and of getting out of the slow-death poverty at the end of the Valley line at Merthyr Tydfil, all of these things were knocked out too. Extinguished for ever.

It wasn't a pretty sight that the world tuned in to on 19 September 1980 in the heat of that early-autumn Los Angeles evening at the back end of round 12.

The great Welsh warrior was quiet now. But the Mexican crowd went mad. Mad because they had thought that here was a challenger so great, so wonderful that he might just take their title back to Wales. They went mad out of sheer relief. They went mad because Johnny Owen, the no-hoper skeleton man from Merthyr Tydfil had very nearly beaten their hero. So they showed no respect when the end came. That wasn't their way.

They shouted and screamed and behaved like the victors in some long-lost medieval battle. They wanted a head on a pole or a platter, or something to that effect. They rained down cups of urine on the now crowded ring. They fought with the Welshmen in the crowd. They even fought amongst themselves. They were ecstatic and dangerous and relieved it was over.

The officials, woken now from the fighters' hour, had to come to terms with the crowd's collective and precarious elation. In the ring lay the unconscious boxer, by his side the doctor, screaming for salts and stretcher, for medics and oxygen, for space to clear, and shaking his head, as only doctors can, when things are bad.

Dick had tears welling in his eyes. Some were running down his cheeks already. 'My son, my son, my son,' was all he could seem to think of to say. Dai Gardner stood ashen-faced and stunned. His thoughts were equally confused and illogical. 'What have we done? What has been done in this place, on this night, in the name of sport?' And, of course, 'Why?' Nothing seemed to make sense any more.

And above all of this, above the bedlam, the manic media reporters, the flash of the camera lights, the intrusion of the TV anchormen, above all of this stood the glistening, muscle-toned, super-fit but tired-and-tested Mexican champion of the whole wide world, Lupe Pintor. Standing erect. Staring over the prostrate body of his equal, his friend and his blood brother in all of this insanity, Johnny Owen.

Lupe Pintor – victorious, exhausted, respectful, relieved and frightened. Here was the gladiator. Johnny was the gladiator. Los Angeles was the new Rome. And this was the end of the road for them both.

3

THE KID

When Johnny Owen came along there was pride about his being
from Merthyr. Johnny was such a gentle man. A young man who
said, 'Mr This' and 'Mr That'. His attitude was one of polite
determination. It made people like him all the more . . . Other
boxers rarely got above themselves, Johnny certainly never did. He
was the consummate well-brought-up young man. In one sense,
he epitomised Merthyr.

A Merthyr resident reminiscing, 2003

Over most of Great Britain and Northern Ireland it was a crisp and
clear midwinter's day on Saturday, 7 January 1956. Three days earlier,
the country had been deluged in what was reported to have been the
fourth-wettest day since records began. So the sunshine came as a
blessed relief, even if it was a bit cold.

Popular music, sport, movies and politics dominated the society of
the time, much as they do today, though their public delivery would
have been vastly different in comparison to our crazy, hyped-up, digital
way of doing things. Living was a little slower, a little easier back then,
the pace of life a little less hectic. The presentation of leisure-time
activities, news and sports a little more innocent and naive. For all that,
things were no less important than we think they are now.

JOHNNY OWEN

Bill Haley and His Comets sat at number one in the pop charts that January and there was much talk in the newspapers and on the radio of a young man called Elvis Presley. Change was in the air and on the way. The best film of 1956, with its eight Oscar nominations, was the wonderful adaptation of Jules Verne's *Around the World in 80 Days*. In politics and current affairs, Anthony Eden was busily preparing to commit political suicide over Suez. Highlights in the world of sport included the seventh Winter Olympic Games due to be held in southern Italy. The various British teams readied themselves to compete, but with little hope of any major success. Some things rarely change. The undisputed heavyweight champion of the world was Rocky Marciano, while the brilliant French-Algerian boxer Robert Cohen held the title of world bantamweight champion.

On that same day in 1956, Dick and Edith Owens celebrated the birth of their new son, John Richard Owens. He was born at Gwaunfarren Maternity Hospital in Merthyr Tydfil, South Wales. He would not become Johnny Owen until he graduated to the rank of 'professional boxer' many years later and adopted the pseudonym. The proud parents lived at 12 Heol Bryn Selu in a small, council-rented property on the large Gellideg housing estate above the town. John was their fourth child. The couple had married eight years earlier on 1 May 1948 after a brief, whirlwind courtship. It was all very exciting and all very right. They were both 21 years old at the time. John Owens was born into a close-knit, working-class family. Eventually, there would be eight children – five boys and three girls. His four brothers and three sisters – Philip, Marilyn, Vivian, Kelvin, Susan, Dilwyn and Shereen – all survive their more famous and illustrious brother.

As a child, John was quiet, shy, kind, unassuming and generous. These are not behavioural characteristics normally associated with potential boxers. Sporting champions are rarely shy, unassuming and quiet. It got worse. John could top those personality traits with a physical appearance that again did not lend itself to promoting the idea of a future sporting star. He was frail, pale and skinny. No one of sound mind and judgement could have predicted that this bashful, slender diminutive kid would one day become a world champion boxer. Only a supreme optimist, being carried away shouting and screaming by men in white coats, could have suggested such an outcome at the time. And no one did. So, from the outset (and from the outside), John Owens seemed destined for anything but professional Championship boxing. The comment, 'He doesn't look like a boxer, does he?' would follow him throughout his life. But the young Owens was a great deal tougher than he looked.

As a young boy, John attended Gellideg Infant and Junior School and then, later on, as he grew into adolescence, Georgetown County Secondary Modern School. Both schools are based in Merthyr Tydfil. His annual reports were always steady and never really above par, but he was a creative child with a vivid imagination and a wonderful, slow, dry sense of humour which would occasionally emerge when something amused him or took his fancy. John Owens was a healthy child, good natured, happy and mild-mannered. His school reports more or less always said the same thing. 'John is quiet, very well behaved, 100 per cent interested and always gives of his best.' He was not exactly lighting up the world back then, but he was liked and respected by those who knew him.

John used to love shopping and often set off around Merthyr Tydfil shopping centre, chirping breezy hellos to all and sundry, as happy as you like, picking up the groceries for the family. Those who remember that time say he was a good shopper. Always looking for bargains. Saving a penny here, a halfpenny there. With the family grown to eight children, John's contribution with the daily chores was invaluable. As you can imagine, with eight kids it would have been a hugely busy household.

John loved all of this busyness and the large family he had been born into. He had been very lucky. What better start to life can there be for a young boy than to be free, light of heart and spirit, and part of a true and loving family? John, then, for the whole world to see, was a happy child. Soon after he started school for the first time, the family moved from the old house, which was getting cramped for space, in Heol Bryn Selu, to a brand new and slightly bigger one down the road in Bryn

Padell on the same housing estate overlooking the town. John Richard Owens was to grow up and realise many a dream and ambition in that new house, and make both himself and it famous along the way. As I write, his proud parents, Dick and Edith Owens, still live there.

John Owens' mother, Edith, was born in Merthyr Tydfil of Welsh and Irish ancestry. Her father was a farmer from Lydney in the Forest of Dean. Dick's family and ancestors were originally tempted away from Llanidloes in mid-Wales. Both families moved to the Merthyr Tydfil area mainly for economic reasons: there were more jobs and more benefits on offer in the industrial south of Wales. A new era of steel, iron and coal production had been ushered in across the whole country and South Wales in particular was affected more than most by the absolute changes the new industries brought with them. For workers, at least in theory, it was a boom time.

The revolution in industry caused by the Industrial Revolution meant work and with jobs came regular, sustainable incomes. It was a time of great change. In the country and outlying non-industrial areas of Wales, it was becoming very hard to find and maintain a long-term 'proper' job beyond these vast new industries. Men flocked to the new towns in droves from all parts of Great Britain, in many cases exchanging the fresh air of the country for the turgid drudge of the daily slave labour enforced upon them by pitiless governments or Works owners. It was, genuinely and without exaggeration, a tough, hard life in Merthyr Tydfil, but for those who undertook the challenges on offer, it seemed there was no real alternative, no other way. And once you were in, there was no getting out.

The Owens family was no different from hundreds and thousands of other families settling in the area at that time. For those with their fingers on the tills of the Industrial Revolution, these were very exciting and exploitative times. Wealth was there to be created. A whole new social order was being constructed on the back of a grossly underpaid, badly managed workforce, propping up Works owners and a corrupt political system by default. They were to all intents and purposes the slaves of the Industrial Revolution. Great Britain has rarely encouraged fairness in the business of sharing the nation's wealth. From the point of view of those who had to give up their daily existence to dig out coal or work in the oppressive heat and dangerous conditions of the iron and steel works, life was disappointing, sometimes hopeless and almost always very unfair.

In the early days, when the family first moved to the Merthyr area, the Owens clan lived in a place called Penwaunfawr, a small village on what is now the outskirts of the main town of Merthyr Tydfil. There were about 250 houses there. Like so many other new villages in South Wales at that time, it seemed to have risen from almost nothing, out of nowhere, to fit in with the developing and growing economy of the region. Such was the speed of industrial development, towns and villages like Penwaunfawr would often spring up almost overnight. All around these new villages grew great stacks of black, unwanted surplus waste tips, very often courtesy of the 'Dowlais Iron and Steel Works'. Giant, silent mountains of black debris rose out of the ground, forever climbing as more and more waste and dust was daily and endlessly added. Village life was not something one would write home about. It was bleak and dismal, as were the lives of the inhabiting human beings as they quickly became surrounded and shrouded, almost buried, under the big, black industrial dumps. *One day, the most vulnerable would pay the price in order to see these hideous logos of greed removed for ever.*

The villages surrounding Merthyr Tydfil soon melded into each other, losing their natural boundaries as the town exploded with industry, and more and more people settled there. Merthyr grew and grew, and eventually became a more acceptable place to settle. With that acceptance, a thriving town with plenty of shops and social attractions, a town with a character all of its own, was born. People were arriving from all over Europe to work in Merthyr Tydfil and sometimes they would even come from beyond the boundaries of the Continent. The British Empire encouraged workers from all parts of the globe.

John Owens' great-grandmother worked underground. His great-grandfather, William John Robins, who came from Aberystwyth, worked in the iron works and fought in the boxing booths in a small district at the top of Merthyr town. From what is known of him, hearsay mostly, he was a pretty decent boxer. John's grandmother worked in the iron works cleaning out the ovens and his grandfather, Dick Owens, was a good footballer and a runner.

John Owens loved to run, too. He liked the isolation and enjoyed the time to think out there on the road. He could have excelled as a runner. In many senses, he was made to run. He looked, for all the world, very much the archetypal long-distance runner, with the long body and skinny frame. It was a sport he might well have associated himself with and the only other sport he'd ever have contemplated competing in. But at eight years old, like his great-grandfather before him, John Owens' interest was drawn to boxing. There was never any competition as to which path he would take from that point on. The moment of epiphany had arrived.

With that interest in mind, records show that he went with his elder brother Vivian to Merthyr Amateur Boxing Club for the first time in the spring of 1962. Vivian had been working out and training there for quite a while. He was streetwise, experienced at the club and knew his way around. John had taken the first adventurous steps on the road to becoming a sporting champion.

Unbeknown to his schoolmates, John quickly and quietly began to make a name for himself in Welsh amateur boxing circles. He wasn't to electrify those that first saw him box, but he showed great talent and resilience, and, from the outset, he had a big heart. It was clear he loved to box from day one. He had found something. The first step to success in any medium is discovery, finding what you love. The next is immersion in that love. That was the way for John Owens: he would immerse himself in the work and study of his new-found craft. Even at that early age, he had the work-ethic bug. It would be the same work ethic that would much later help form the finished article – Johnny Owen.

John had never excelled academically and was always unlikely to do so. Like so many working-class kids of that time, he soon found out that the opportunities mouthed by those that ruled were not quite replicated in the classroom. As a young kid growing up in Merthyr

Tydfil, you had to be really interested to get on academically. Frankly, John was not that interested, which was not that unusual. In fact, hardly anyone growing up with him at that time was bothered much about school. Mostly, everyone knew his or her place. Life was more or less mapped out for you from an early age. As a kid, you just shrugged your shoulders and got on with it. On the sports field, aside from his love of running, John Owens was run-of-the-mill, ordinary. He was not for Cardiff Arms Park, the then home of Welsh rugby, or Lord's Cricket Ground. But in the local boxing gymnasium, his ordinariness was set aside. He was becoming something of an enigma. Quiet and reserved outside the ring, a determined and fierce exponent within it, John Richard Owens had found his way.

The young, enthusiastic boxer was immediately accepted into the club. There was a great atmosphere at Merthyr Amateur Boxing Club around that time. A lot of hope was held out for the future and all concerned seemed to have plenty to shout about. The boxing was competitive and fair, and every challenger would give of his personal best for the club. Competitive bouts were regular and well organised, and each year culminated in the staging of the Welsh Amateur Championships. In those days, the competition was a special event and would usually be held on a Saturday. Because of the huge interest, along with the paperwork and organisation, it had to be an all-day affair. Very often it turned into an almost 24-hour affair.

The contestants would weigh in at around nine o'clock in the morning. On most occasions, there would be 300 to 400 boys to get onto the scales. They were matched according to their weight and all particulars had to be written down in duplicate, sometimes triplicate. It was a tiresome and mundane task, but one that had to be addressed judiciously and managed properly at all times. The boxing itself would normally start at around one o'clock in the afternoon. The fights would be well planned out and all the young competitors excellently looked after.

Very often, the final bouts would not finish until one o'clock or later the following morning. But it was always worth the extra effort. Everyone would have a great time, and the whole event served Wales and the community well. The main purpose was also well served in that the experience was invaluable to the young competitors involved. All of this excitement and exhilaration was wondrous experience for the young John Owens. He loved everything about his chosen sport. From the smell of the wintergreen massage oil in the dressing-room to the sound of the final bell, the raising of the arms in victory and the planning for the next bout, along with all points in between. It fascinated the young boxer. He felt he belonged. In boxing and around boxing, John Owens was at home.

He was his sport just as so many other champions were before him. He was in love with boxing as much as Muhammad Ali ever was. As Maradona or Pele must have been with their discovery of the beautiful game, so John was with boxing. As Ginger McCain was with the wonder and fame of the Grand National and Red Rum, so John was with the ring and the training gymnasiums and the dressing-rooms and the fight nights. There was nothing else for John Owens. And anyone who was around him then could tell that boxing was to be his chosen craft.

All went perfectly and gloriously well for him too as his introductory phase in the sport continued. John won a few bouts and started to build up quite a name for himself as a new talent and, of course, winning makes everything right, so the young boy soon relaxed into thinking winning would always be his destiny. It is an easy mistake to make in sport. Overconfidence means defeat almost every time. Setbacks in sport are never far away and tests of character for any serious sportsman, no matter how young or old, experienced or inexperienced they might be, are always around the corner. John's first genuine setback occurred when he fought at Cymmer Afan, in the Afan Valley, near Port Talbot in the industrial south of Wales. It was then that everyone began to see in the young John Owens something they hadn't known or realised fully before. The quiet boy was very determined. And in that determination lay the seeds of the champion.

The boxing bout in question was a strong and competitive fight between John and a boy whose name has unfortunately long since disappeared from record. According to those present, the fight seemed to go well for John. He'd put up a good performance, was confident of the result and convinced he had won, but the referee's verdict went to his opponent. John stormed out of the ring and refused to return for his runner's-up certificate. He stayed in the dressing-room, furious with the world, refusing to come out. When finally he was handed the loser's parchment, he threw it away. He didn't want a loser's certificate and made that known to everyone present. He also made it known that he was, from that day on, finished with boxing. That was all he would say on the matter. The stubborn young boy had spoken! It's hard to believe, but he was just eight years old at the time and already displaying the competitive instincts of a true champion.

Around this time, John and his father, Dick Owens, would walk the mountains behind the old town of Merthyr Tydfil. Dick knew his boxing and he knew his son. So it is not out of the bounds of imagination to assume that he would have known his son had talent even then. He would have known and he would have confronted John with that knowledge. If John was to continue boxing, then he would have to play the game, and accept defeat and victory as one and the same. Dick Owens would one day become the young man's trainer, his mentor and his closest friend. Maybe even then, during those mountain walks, plans were being laid for the future. We can never know for certain. John might well have been ticked off for the bad behaviour he displayed at that losing bout. Then perhaps his father would have left him to contemplate defeat alone. Who could know for certain? It would be the act of a shrewd and wise trainer to point his protégé in the right direction early on. And Dick Owens was indeed a talented trainer.

Picture this skinny, pale-faced eight-year-old boxer staring down from the small brown-green hillside overlooking the tough and grey, iron, steel and coal town. Picture him burning with steely ambition. Could it be at this time, after this early setback, at this place, that John Richard Owens decided his future path? Was this perhaps the moment he dedicated himself to boxing and to becoming a champion? Was it *there* he vowed to give 110 per cent at all times and to never give in to any opponent? And was it there that the resolve to try to win and try to never lose, ever again, was forged? We will never know, but we can guess it may well have been.

What we do know is that the Merthyr Tydfil that the eight-year-old boxer looked down upon that day had seen many a tough individual in its time. You had to be strong to live there, even in the 1960s, when the Klondike spirit forged in the white heat of the Industrial Revolution was sadly waning. John belonged to this town's spirit and the town's history made John's steely resolve.

Merthyr Tydfil and John Richard Owens were made for each other.

4

MERTHYR

The old mountain fighters are almost all gone, all but died out now. Many of them used to come up from the mines and fight bare-knuckle on the mountains that surrounded the town. They would sometimes dig two small pits waist high, side by side, the idea being that whoever went into them to fight stayed there to the 'death'. There is one fighter who is still remembered from the bare-knuckle era. His name was Redman Coalman. He was born in 1874 and lived in Merthyr all his life.

Redman Coalman was a terrible, fierce man, no gentleman and no respecter of age, class or gender. He was the most celebrated bare-knuckle fighter of his day. A champion of sorts, he was known by every police officer in Merthyr, and by every local judge and magistrate. His favourite trick was to stand on the bridge in town and charge a toll for people crossing it. Didn't bother him if you were man or woman, if you didn't pay you had to fight him. And fight him they did. By the thousand.

He died in 1927 at Merthyr's Workhouse Infirmary aged 53. They still talk about him to this day. His legend lives on (as they say!). He was the first fighting son of Merthyr Tydfil to be really remembered.

The image of Merthyr Tydfil as a straight-talking, street-fighting, post-industrial sprawl has been quietly cultivated over the years, mainly by outsiders. More often than not, visitors would report back telling of a 'grim community hanging on by its fingertips'(hanging on to what is anyone's guess). They'd tell of a town dangling precariously on a mountain-top, where it rained all the time and snowed in the winter; a place of beer-drinking sessions of epic proportions and of fighting in the streets and bars. Apparently, there is always fighting in the streets and bars of Merthyr Tydfil. Scrapping after a few pints is the heritage of all rough-and-ready industrial towns. The booze must have its say. The frustration of a life of work without end, imprisoned by the manufacturing of steel or coal or tin has to vent its spleen somewhere. And very often drink becomes boss and the fist does the talking.

This understandable legacy, a hangover from an almost bygone industrial age, is not unique to Merthyr Tydfil. It is the case in almost all towns and cities influenced by heavy industry. Fighting for your rights goes with the territory of the frontier spirit. For hard-working men and women, it is laudable and, although it may sometimes seem 'uncivilised' to the untrained, mild-mannered foreigner, it is very often excusable. This tough image, however, hides much.

Taken at face value, this simplistic version of Merthyr Tydfil is easy to digest, but scratch beneath the surface and you will soon clearly see it for what it is: superficial stuff, hot air, propaganda. The Merthyr fighting spirit goes a lot deeper than a few punch-ups, mythical tales of bare-knuckle fighting, and hard men and women. Like so many post-industrial towns, Merthyr Tydfil has a proud and unique past. Not too far beneath that rough, brash surface, beneath that reckless veneer, lies a rare, compassionate and much-deeper fighting spirit.

Merthyr Tydfil's contribution to social change and fair conditions for human beings wherever they are forced to work or live in deprivation and poverty is legendary in Wales and beyond. This was another fight. Another kind of fight altogether. But the people of Merthyr Tydfil were up for it. Someone had to do it and Merthyr was one of the towns that gladly stood on the front line. It blazed a trail for social justice and fair play for all, and would always stand up for the weaker man or woman against an authoritative State or corporate system. Merthyr Tydfil was to the naturally conservative politicians of Great Britain and its Empire a great big blasted pain in the neck.

The inhabitants of Merthyr Tydfil fought against industrial exploiters and oppression; they fought for social change, decent wages and better conditions, and housing and health care for their people. They fought for recognition by the trades unions, for shorter hours of work, improved social security benefits, help in old age and longer holidays in the sun for those who spent near-lifetimes in the darkness of the pit. They fought for pennies an hour more in the pay packet, representation in Parliament, equal rights for women and the safety of children. These are the other kinds of fights, much more powerful battles. Battles the town was well equipped to deal with.

In the evolution of any industrial town, the fight between the workers and the owners of their labour will always lead to social change. It has to because those who purchase labour, by instinct if not definition, seek only to carve out profits. That is their principal motive for being in business. Whether they carve those profits out on the bodies of those they exploit or not means little to them. So, those selling their labour have to fight. They have to fight for all the things that Merthyr Tydfil workers and their families fought for because, as all workers in this situation quickly find out, no one is given decent conditions by right. It rarely happens in this world based on capital, where profit seems to be God Almighty. The standard rule when dealing with business is that you must ask for a little above what you need and then 'negotiate'. Where that leads is something else – as Oliver Twist discovered to his and our mutual benefit.

The people of Merthyr Tydfil did a lot of asking, a lot of fighting and a lot of negotiating and, in the end, their belligerence and courage helped to change the world. These are the 'other' fights. These are the other battles that the grey, hard-bitten Welsh valley town is famous for. Confrontations and conflicts which, if they had been totally successful, might well have tamed the fights and battles in the streets of the irrepressible old town. But then, if they had been totally successful, the character of the damn place would have disappeared, wouldn't it? Life is not a pleasurable experience without conflict or struggle. Heck, the town was born out of fight!

Merthyr Tydfil nestles in the north of the River Taff valley; next stop, the stunningly beautiful Brecon Beacons, the small mid-Wales mountain range so popular with tourists. It is often cold in the summer and quite warm in the winter and, due to its location and height, the mountains surrounding it ensure that the ground is watered regularly. Ah, yes, the Welsh rain. Where would we be without it? To the south of the Beacons and Merthyr lies what remains of the harsh reality of industrial Wales along with the nation's exquisite and very modern capital city, Cardiff.

Merthyr Tydfil owes its name to Tudful, the daughter of Brychan, Prince of Brycheiniog, who was slain by the marauding Picts in the fifth century at the site of the parish church. She was subsequently canonised and the site on which she was slain became known as *Martyr Tudful*, morphing into Merthyr Tydfil as the years passed by. That first 'scrap' on the site of the old church gave the town its name and, many believe, its wonderfully anarchic character.

The Borough of Merthyr Tydfil, as it is officially known, has a population of around 55,000, give or take a few. It extends from Dowlais in the north through Merthyr Town, Troedyrhiw, Aberfan and Merthyr Vale to Treharris, Trelewis and Bedlinog in the south, some ten miles away.

The late twentieth century brought vast improvements in transport infrastructure to Merthyr Tydfil, making it accessible to visitors and allowing its residents to travel to places of which previously they could only have dreamt. Wales's premier cities, Cardiff and Swansea, are but 30 minutes away; Birmingham and London are no more than 2 to 3 hours' travelling time; Cardiff Airport is a mere 30 miles from the town centre. Merthyr Tydfil is now a truly international town. And what a town!

Socialist ideas and ideals also flourished in the first half of the twentieth century in the town. It was the place of Paul Robeson visits, of fire-and-brimstone chapels, and of a deeply committed community spirit. The place where, in 1801, two miners were hung for fighting to avoid starvation after food riots took place in Merthyr Town. The place where, in 1831, a four-day stand-off by workers fighting for better pay and conditions against government troops led to twenty-one deaths. The workers won in the end. And at the height of the Depression, in 1935, scores of women stormed the National Assistance Board offices in Merthyr Town and destroyed the records that set out to deprive them of financial support. These are but tiny examples of the fighting nature of the place.

Merthyr Tydfil is one of the key towns in the rise and history of the Labour movement of Great Britain and Northern Ireland. Here, they fought tooth and nail to help give birth to the British Labour Party. No fewer than three great leaders of the Party have a deep intellectual and personal bond with the town. Keir Hardie, whom many regard as the founding father of the British Labour movement and the Party's first leader, was Member of Parliament for Merthyr Tydfil. Hardie, a Scotsman, found a new spiritual home in his constituency. He found in Merthyr a place that epitomised what his party stood for, a place teeming with ideas for social reform. In the 1980s, a further two Labour politicians with deep roots in industrial Wales and powerful connections with Merthyr Tydfil became leaders of the Labour Party: the impressive firebrand Neil Kinnock was one; the wholly cerebral and genuine gentleman of the left, Michael Foot, the other. Many, many more unsung (and sung, for that matter!) fighters for human rights and better conditions were either born in Merthyr Tydfil or found compassionate support for their causes there.

These are but a few of the many examples of the good people and the tough fights the town attracted and participated in. Chosen tiny examples. A fraction of the reality of Merthyr Tydfil's fights for social justice and better conditions for its hard-pressed people. These confrontations were surely equally, or much more so, important to the make-up and legend of Merthyr Tydfil as the street fighting and Saturday night, post-booze-up curry-house brawls ever were.

But the bigger-picture fights, the fights at the highest political level, are now almost all in the past. At least they seem to be for the moment, anyway. The world of the twenty-first century is a new and in some ways more frightening and complex place. The reign of Margaret Thatcher's Government ushered in the end of the industrial age. In the 1980s, it brought so cruelly to a close the old way of doing things and ensured the death of fair play, and the game played by the old rules. The miners' strike in the mid-1980s almost killed Merthyr Tydfil dead. We are in another era now. The era of pointless property ownership, stocks and shares manipulation, the Internet, golf courses in place of coal tips, Sunday lunch in restaurants, satellite TV and the European Union with its freedom to travel and work, and its new money. And, of course, New Labour. There have been so many changes since that last great boxing battle of Johnny Owen's short young life took place in September 1980. Being in Merthyr Tydfil now is almost like being in a foreign land. Everything is altered beyond belief.

So maybe that gives us a clue as to what Merthyr is hanging on to by its fingertips? Its whole history has been forged out of a giant scrap against the odds, against the demons of oppression and hard times. Maybe Merthyr is really hanging on by its fingertips to days gone by when things 'meant' something? Maybe the future bothers its inhabitants? Maybe they feel that all they have fought for, over all these years, will ultimately be seen to have been in vain, all lost? Maybe the old town still has a sense of community denied to those 'other' towns which have now moved on and into the 'modern' age? Maybe way back there, in the past, lies their place of certainty, their identity? Merthyr Tydfil has a lot to lose. Perhaps more so than most towns. Merthyr fought for what it believed in and to lose that sense of belief could mean losing everything. So they hang on.

Merthyr is not politically correct. It has its own ambassadors, its own inhabitants, acting as spin doctors in punch-ups all over Wales. There they escalate the 'hard as nails and couldn't care less' myth tenfold. But it isn't the truth. Don't let them con you. There is a huge welcome in this hillside. There always has been.

It escapes no one that this harsh industrial town finds itself at the end of the line, the Valley Railway Line. As ironic a fate as any town could ever have had bestowed upon it. 'You can't make it up, can you!' one wag in the town library said to me, casting a satirical eye around as another grey night fell on the old iron town. And into this melting pot came the sport of boxing and the great fighters. They and their sport evolved in Merthyr because their society demanded it. They were a reflection of those fighting for social justice. 'I demand you notice me fighting for my life in a boxing ring because if you notice me, you will notice my kind, and if you notice them, you will see their injustice,' is what I feel they might have been saying. These men who entered the boxing ring in Merthyr Tydfil were carrying huge messages to the world. And the town became a boxing institution at home and abroad.

In the end, no one can deny Merthyr its right to be the boxing capital of Wales. That much is absolutely true. Merthyr Tydfil as a place for boxers to learn and grow, and become champions is up there fighting it out with probably the East End of London, Belfast or Glasgow as the boxing capital of the whole of the United Kingdom. Fighting, in one guise or another, is in the blood of everyone born in Merthyr Tydfil. It has to be. It's locked up in the genes, part of the evolutionary process of belonging to this great town. The Owens family go back a long way in Merthyr. They were a family of fighters and survivors. They still are. It's in their blood.

Four truly great fighters came from this place (well, three from Merthyr itself, one other came from the neighbouring Rhondda Valley). They were Jimmy Wilde, Tommy Farr, Eddie Thomas and Howard Winstone. All gave something to the character of Johnny Owen, and all are necessary as folk heroes and champions to encourage and inspire young boxers, to make the traumatic and difficult journey from great hope to champion worthwhile. All four share with Johnny Owen a vast resource of a very rare commodity: courage.

Jimmy Wilde was Johnny Owen's hero and remains a boxing legend. The 'Ghost with a Hammer in his Hand' lost only 3 of 148 fights in a 13-year career. The Merthyr boxer is regarded worldwide as the greatest flyweight of all time. In fact, many believe Jimmy Wilde is the greatest fighter of all time.

Tommy Farr, 'the Pride of Tonypandy', will always be remembered for taking the legendary Joe Louis the full distance of 15 rounds in their Heavyweight World Championship title clash at Madison Square Garden in New York. No one before had come so close to beating the great 'Brown Bomber'.

The statue of the supreme and classy boxer, Eddie Thomas, stands near to the statue of Johnny Owen in Merthyr Tydfil town centre. This wonderful local champion went on to train another world champion from Merthyr, the enigmatic and multi-talented Howard Winstone.

Johnny Owen fits in neatly with these four greats and, as we will see from his career path, he deserves all the accolades bestowed on them too. Johnny Owen, from his first amateur fight to his final professional fight, was to become a great boxer in his own right.

As Jimmy Wilde did before him, Johnny Owen was to prove that size and a lack of academic aptitude matter little in the fierce competitive world of big-money professional sports. A huge heart, a bag full of courage and the biggest dream of all can carry a resilient and determind man an awful long way.

Johnny Owen, the boxer, had all of these qualities and ambitions, and more. He had a secret weapon, too. For he was also blessed with every single one of the fighting qualities Merthyr Tydfil could bestow upon him. Johnny Owen's prowess as a boxer could not be put down to his supreme skills alone; the old town had a bit to do with it too.

5

MEXICO!

Poor Mexico! So far from God, so close to the United States.
Porfirio Diaz, Mexican President (1830–1915)

There is nothing more depressing in the world of travelling (well, there are, there are lots of things, but, for now, there aren't) than a long-haul flight. The experience begins with the realisation that the continuous drone of the jumbo jet never goes away. It's there for the duration and there's no hiding-place. Then begins, in the strangely cramped and sometimes hostile environment, the irritatingly baffling clock-watching (done by all) and, more recently, gazing at the 'computerised' journey as it happens on screen. The cartoon aeroplane hovering slowly across the Atlantic tortures in its speed of travel even more than the clock does by its lack of ambition for haste. Then there's the inability to get some decent sleep, the awful in-flight 'entertainment', and the overwhelming sense that this might just be your last foray, your last adventure (this thing will become a statistic, we are all doomed, aren't we?). All will conspire to make life very uneasy for the long-haul traveller. No matter how hard you try to work it all out, time rarely passes swiftly by.

You would generally board the flight and settle in. Aisle space fought for, hand luggage packed away first. Then take a drink, maybe have a read, and then devour and hope to survive meal number one. After the meal, it's time for a movie. The lights would dim and the thin three-quarter blankets would make an appearance and an attempt at sleep would be made. This attempt at slumber would almost certainly be timed to coincide with the hitting of 'nasty' turbulence and you'd think, 'Damn!', knowing full well sleep would not come easy now. So you'd wait a while, and look at your watch and at the cartoon aeroplane. 'My goodness, but we've travelled another quarter of an inch! Won't be long now!' After a period of renewed settling, you'd try again for the elusive nap you'd been promising yourself you were going to take since the previous night, come what may. Then you'd look at your watch again. Only ten hours to go. Ten! Mexico City can't be that far away, surely?

I think I was the first of our small travelling group to wake. I looked at my watch (yes, again!). Yeuch! At least another four hours to go. I'd been sleeping, I knew that, but not too well. I knew that too. It was still dark in the cabin: dark and silent inside, dark and eerie outside. A few of my fellow passengers were reading or chatting, but not many. Most were trying out the notion of slumber. Dylan might have been asleep. I couldn't really tell. His eyes were covered by a socket-less mask, one item in a bag of 'must-haves' presented to us all with a smile by the all-frills airline staff shortly after take off. Anyway, Dylan might have been awake, but not wanting to see anyone. Perhaps he was 'in a meeting'. Dick Owens stirred in the seat next to me. A nice Dutch air steward appeared. 'Menu, sir?' she smiled. I took it, chose the chicken and passed the menu to my fellow traveller from Merthyr Tydfil. He looked like he needed time to wake up. The grunts gave it away. Grunts and hair all over the place give the game away every time. We were 3 hours and 50 minutes out of Mexico City now. Not long to go. Doesn't time fly when you're having fun?

Come to think of it, I had slept quite well. I knew this because I had dreamt. And I had dreamt about boxing. I had dreamt in black and white and with full commentary. I'd been part of something, something from a long-gone era, something off the scale of my understanding. There were two principal boxers. Both were young and white with greased-back black hair. They were overseen by a shadowy third man, presumably the referee. The bell clanged loud and clear, ceremonially summoning the boxers and the spectators to join in the play. The bell represented something. Authority, time and place perhaps. I don't know. I then witnessed the 'dream' fight at close quarters, but I was never able to recognise any of the participants. They were familiar, they gave off familiar vibes, and they were right up front before me, but they were not prepared to give up their identities. It puzzled me. I glanced across at Dick Owens and was about to tell him of my dream when I remembered a recent discovery I had made, and felt for a connection.

As I made my way through the writing process for this book and in preparation for the documentary, I had found out that my great-uncle, long deceased, Will (Billy) Hughes, from Aberdare, had been a boxer. He had been trained by his brother, a much older man than he. His name was Gruff Hughes, from my home town, Kidwelly, in west Wales. In later years, Gruff was to be my grandfather. The two men – one having fought on the battlefields of the First World War, the other fighting on the economic battlefield of 1920s Britain – tried to box their way out of the Depression and the unemployment catastrophe that surrounded them at that time. Gruff was the trainer, Billy the fighter. One night, in the last round of a 'money' bout 'up North', Billy Hughes was knocked to the floor. He died quite soon afterwards. As Dick Owens once told me, 'You live that moment over and over. It never leaves you.' So it must have been for my grandfather, who never mentioned to me that he once trained his brother to box. I knew little of this family tale till I began to work with the story of Johnny Owen. I am hugely grateful I found it out. Now I was dreaming of it. It was there, in me. For some reason, boxing was there in my genetic memory, waiting to be resurrected or downloaded, waiting to be rescued. Maybe there was a film there, a movie script perhaps, based in the 1920s. *Lightning Billy!* – now there's a thought.

Dick was now fully roused and we began to talk. First, we chatted about the flight. Normal stuff about sleep and food and comfort, and then we wondered about Dylan, our partially silent director, and whether or not he'd wake up at all during the flight. I said, 'Be assured, when the food comes he will surface.' The food duly arrived and he did. Food is so important in the world of television and film. They eat and think and discuss, and eat and think and discuss, and then one day after years of going through the motions of eating and thinking and discussing, someone does something. It takes a while to take that in. It's so unexpected. So, flying here to a place to actually do something, to actually film something, took a good bit of getting used to.

We talked about Mexico City over the meal. Talked of the Mexico we'd read about. The Mexico from the brochure conveniently tucked into the basket on the rear of the seat in front of us. 'Mexico,' it said, 'has a long and glorious history, and a diversity of landscape and culture that will provide endless fascination to the traveller.' Dick felt the blurb was as clear as mud. This was not the Mexico a boxer would have known anything about, one could be certain of that. It certainly was not the Mexico I'd researched in the context of boxing and boxers. To survive in Mexico City as a fighter, you had to be tough. Mexico City is mean and hostile. 'Down there [I pointed, though we were still hundreds of miles away from being over the city], to box is to command respect,' I said. Respect is a big word in Mexico City.

I told Dick of my dream and of the coincidence of finding out about my great-uncle and his brother, and their 1920s boxing adventure. It seemed to mirror much of what we were doing right now and would certainly tap into many of the things he had experienced. I explained there was a lack of information on the ground regarding Billy Hughes's history as a boxer. Dick listened to what I had to say, understood, and promised to try to get more information for me about the origins and history of my great-uncle's boxing record on our return home. He knew one or two people who knew a thing or two about the history of boxing. He'd sort something out.

As our meal was cleared away, I looked across the aisle. Dylan had gone back to sleep. Or at least was pretending to be asleep. I hoped he was. There are some people – lucky souls they are too – that can sleep just like that, on demand. I am not one of them. Nor was Dick Owens. But he had been dreaming, too. Not as he slept, but generally so. Dreaming of monuments and resolution. Dreaming of Merthyr Tydfil and his Johnny.

He began to tell me about one of his great dreams. He wanted desperately to see a statue of Johnny Owen, carved in his honour and erected in his home town of Merthyr Tydfil. He'd like to see that more that anything before he left this unforgiving earth. He fancied it to stand at the corner of Bethesda Street in the town precinct, with Johnny Owen facing home and Gellideg. They had been collecting money all over the Valleys and in Merthyr Tydfil, and organising events and social occasions for some time now, for just this purpose. A fund had been set up and it looked like they would be able to raise the money, and go ahead with commissioning the project this very year. He asked what I thought about his asking Lupe Pintor to come and unveil the monument, should the statue project come to fruition, should he and Pintor hit it off. If they got on well at the meeting scheduled for a few days' time in Mexico City, he would have the opportunity to ask. I thought it a fabulous idea.

What better way could there be of demonstrating forgiveness, understanding and honour, and of showing the world how boxing is and how boxers really are? I urged him to continue that train of thought. If he felt it right at the time, then he should ask Pintor outright. He wanted Johnny to stand for ever and be recognised as one of Merthyr Tydfil's finest sons. It was a terrific idea. If Lupe Pintor agreed and travelled to South Wales to unveil the statue in honour of Johnny Owen, then he would complete a great circle and end a very painful journey for all concerned. If the opportunity arose and he felt that things had gone well enough, he would ask Pintor. He had made up his mind. I felt that he would get on well with Lupe Pintor. I couldn't envisage a reason for him not to. Though, of course, I had nothing to base my assessment on.

It was to be a big week for Johnny Owen's father. He was about to spend an awfully long time being filmed and interviewed, and hauled around Mexico City. Interminable hours would be wasted patiently waiting for something to happen, then, when it happened, only to be told in an instant that it was over, but then again he'd have done a lot of that in the world of boxing. In heavy training, fighters live in dimensions of boredom others cannot begin to contemplate. It's quite similar really. Aside from all that stuff, which to Dick was largely irrelevant, something that was far more important to him was looming large.

I would guess the most important and pressing concern on his mind that evening, as we came in to land at Mexico City International Airport, would have been the meeting about to be approved with the former world bantamweight champion Lupe Pintor. Confirmation aside, the two men were due to get together on the coming Wednesday. We arrived on the Sunday. It would be a nervy wait for the man from Merthyr Tydfil. None of us associated with this drama, none of us accompanying Dick on this genuinely heroic adventure of his, could begin to understand what kinds of memories were being brought to the fore. We had absolutely no idea what this trip was doing to him or doing for him. How could we? Also, no one had yet raised the spectre of the aftermath. What if it all went wrong? A lot of damage could be being done. The man we would meet in Mexico City would indeed have much to contribute to the outcome of the story we were now all involved in. That much was clear.

It was time to pause our conversation. Time to get some shut-eye prior to landing. The week we had first mused about almost two years previously, then discussed in depth as the musings developed and possible ideas took hold, then with the documentary film's producers had planned to fruition, was about to commence. It was time now to take a deep breath. In that breath, sleep came once again. When you need it, it disowns you and when you want to stay focused, it takes over. Sleep is not something we humans control well.

I thought about Johnny Owen now. Johnny – hugely popular, slow-witted, honest and charming – was Merthyr Tydfil's and Wales's great hope, a real and genuine sporting hero. The big-hearted bantamweight champion of Britain, Europe and the Commonwealth, who somehow lifted us all above the gloom as he carried our hopes and aspirations a little further, cheering us in his heroic exploits. I thought about how different he looked from other boxers. He'd looked more like a jockey than a boxer: small, very thin with anaemic-like, marble-white skin, grey sticky-out ears, wide, wide eyes and a long smile that ran from ear to ear. I thought about him running, ghost-like, through Merthyr Tydfil.

Johnny was always running. He'd perfected his balance, with his legs and lungs working together in unison, in an equal state of exertion. Johnny had no trouble there. He loved running as much as he loved boxing. He was a perfectly attuned athlete in harmony with his body.

In what seemed liked hours, but was probably seconds later, I was awoken by the same air steward who had brought the menu to me earlier. I had dozed off. 'Please adjust your seat to the upright position and fasten your seat belt. We are preparing to land.' It was a nice way to be brought back to consciousness. The plane was making its descent. Dylan was wide awake and talking across the aisle to a very animated Dick Owens. Through the cabin window of the now strangely comfortable jet, one could see the mass of buildings that made up Mexico City. I sat upright and looked at the ground below in awe. It seemed there was no horizon. Just houses. Houses and lights.

Twenty million people lived down there. There were no real skyscrapers. One or two bigger buildings stood out, but they were few and far between. There were literally just human dwellings – houses, shacks and tents, and mansions for the rich (probably) – and business buildings of all colours and sizes, and churches and chapels galore. From where I looked, there seemed no end to the human rubble. Electricity burned like it was going out of fashion. The whole mass of earth below was lit up and stunning, and a little frightening too. The city stretched out endlessly. I searched my pockets for the paperwork I had meticulously hidden about my person and needed to display to get past immigration, through Customs and into the country. It was time to relax and wait for the ground to meet us.

Dick Owens sat back in his seat. Dylan waved a cheery hello to me across the aisle, a kind of 'good morning' here in the middle of the night, and then once more we fell into a tranquil mode, more than likely anticipating a crash landing. The air stewards clipped themselves in. The wheels of the aircraft prepared to be bounced and burned and scorched. The jumbo that had ferried us from Amsterdam to Mexico City, almost silently, it seemed, made its way to the runway.

6

YOUNG AND EASY

The legendary Irish boxer Barry McGuigan was once asked, 'Why are you a boxer?'
He replied, 'I can't be a poet. I can't tell stories.'
Joyce Carol Oates, *On Boxing*

It's great to be young. Great to be young and easy, and know exactly what it is you want to do with your life. For some of us, the revelation never arrives. We never know. We wander around flitting from one great idea to the next, wondering what the heck we're on the planet for. It's a sure-fire recipe for getting religion, that. Not knowing what it is you're here on this earth for. For those lucky enough to discover their vocation, normal, accepted good and bad things aside, life is very often a breeze. John Richard Owens knew exactly what he was about. Those boxing gloves fitted him perfectly. And now, fully recovered from his upset at losing a fight, realising that one could not win them all, all of the time, he started to train once more. It was an exciting time for the young man. He was to work out and train hard without pause for the next 14 years. Hard work was to be his philosophy. Hard work plus talent and determination equals success – it is the secret of life itself, and the young boy had stumbled upon it early.

John recovered quickly from the setback of losing at Cymmer Afan and was soon back in the ring. He was a quick learner and the Merthyr Tydfil youth set-up was fast becoming an outstanding and famous boxing institution throughout Wales and the West Country of England. Many of the youngsters in training had the makings of future champions. The idea of being around future Championship contenders rubbed off on the younger, newer boxers. It gave them a lift, gave them confidence. In this atmosphere, John felt that he too could one day be talked of as a possible future champion. He felt at home at the club, he enjoyed every second of his time there, it was exactly what he needed. He was very aware that he was indeed a lucky lad to be a part of something so worthwhile.

Another stroke of luck befell the young boxer when his father started a training career of his own. Dick Owens began by working with his sons, training them, all of whom enjoyed the sport and were keen young fighters. Although Dick would treat all his boys equally, from the outset it was clear that John was different. He was already showing himself a notch above the ordinary and was more than just a good, keen fighter. John had class, that indefinable quality, and it had shown itself early, as it very often does. Class is the one thing that sport requires from its top participants in order to continue and to create new and purposeful interest. Class is what sporting stars are all about. Class in those sporting stars is what generates sporting wealth. And you've either got class or you ain't! You cannot manufacture it no matter how hard you try. It was that notion of class that allowed John to quickly establish himself ahead of his brothers as the real boxer in the family. He soon became the centre of his father's training attentions.

Everyone, in and out of the ring, and throughout Merthyr Tydfil, soon discovered that John had a second major talent around this time. It came to everyone's attention as part and parcel of his training regime. He could run. He ran for miles. He ran through the town, across the valley, and up the hills and down the dales – everywhere he could. Training this boxer would not be difficult. A large part of the battle involved in training boxers for the ring is getting in the roadwork. It is not the most pleasant of starts to a day, not every boxer's ideal. For John, though, the roadwork was no inconvenience. He loved it. He'd run and run.

It was a good time for the young boy. It was also a good time for John and the family. At school, his reports reflected the pupil well. They said he was a 'quiet, hardworking, and very good-natured and well-behaved pupil'. In the boxing ring, his knowledge and understanding of the fighter's craft began to take shape. John felt at ease with the world even at such a young age. He was happy and had reason to be confident about the future. That confidence sprang from his dreams of boxing success. The great thing about being different, having a direction and being creative, is that you are blessed with the ability to dream big. And John dreamed big. You must be able to dream. That is surely the purpose for all of us. What else is there? It is the only real act of free will most of us will ever encounter. The only act of freedom we can solely control. In that square ring, there is also dignity and a place for freedom of expression. It is a place of skill and guile, a place of the mind. At first glance, it might look like a physical place, but it is not. Boxing is a game of the mind and the fighter with the fastest mind wins.

John was at the beginning of it all, at the start of the dream, in pole position in the adventure. It always seems the case that when someone wants to learn something so badly, they will always find a way to the knowledge they need to advance their cause. The lesson learned through John and many others is simple: once you find out what you want from life, you find out who you are and can enjoy life. Times would not always be good for the young boxer, though. There would be bad news too. The circle never lets any of us off. *The vulnerable and the defenceless were about to pay the price of greed.* A harsh lesson in life was about to reveal itself to the young boxer.

At 9.15 a.m. on Friday, 21 October 1966, the small Welsh community of Aberfan changed for ever. Tragedy struck when a waste tip slid down a mountainside and into the mining village itself. It first destroyed a farm cottage in its path, killing all the occupants, then it headed for the school. Aberfan borders Merthyr Tydfil and is of the same valley. The grief of Aberfan was the grief of all in that valley on that day.

At Pantglas Junior School, the children had returned to their classes after singing 'All Things Bright and Beautiful' at their assembly. It was sunny on the mountain, but foggy in the village, with visibility down to about 50 yards. A gang of maintenance workers on the mountain had seen the slide start, but could not raise the alarm because their telephone cable had been stolen. Down in the village, nobody saw anything, but everybody heard the noise. The slide engulfed the school and about 20 houses in the village before coming to rest. It happened so quickly.

The Aberfan disaster claimed the lives of 144 people, 116 of them schoolchildren. About half of those attending Pantglas Junior School were lost. A generation wiped out for ever. Five of their teachers were killed with them. It was nearly a week before all the bodies were recovered. Blame for the disaster rested squarely on the National Coal Board.

One of the victims, one of the 116 children dead, was Robert Coffee, a friend of young John Owens and a fellow boxer. Robert was just 12 years old. That terrible day brought home to John and those at the Amateur Boxing Club, and everyone in Merthyr Tydfil, indeed around the world, that youth is no evader of death. Young Robert Coffee would never be forgotten. And the lesson that had to be learned from the awfulness of the disaster was that one must get on with living as opposed to getting on with dying. No day must be wasted, no hour sacrificed and no minute tossed aside. It was a lesson that the young John Owens would have understood instinctively.

In the seven years after the disaster at Aberfan, John's concentration on developing his chosen craft intensified and he became even more dedicated to the sport of amateur boxing. Bout followed bout, training was a 24-hour, 7-days-a-week routine and John ran and ran and ran and ran. By 1973, the 17 year old was super-fit, and lived and breathed boxing. Throughout these formative years, the young Merthyr protégé clearly understood the need for dedication and resolve. He studied his sport from every angle, from fitness to psychology, from the history of boxing to tactical ring awareness and diet. This young boxer wanted something. He believed that in order to get what you want, you have to dedicate life itself to the goal. He knew, as others knew and could so clearly see, that he was talented. He was also well aware that talent in itself was not enough. There had to be more. And so he gave more. The hard work continued, relentlessly, in and out of the ring.

In the ring that year, John had won his way through to the final rounds of the Welsh Junior Championships held at Maerdy in the Rhondda Valley. He was successful and won the bout, but not in the manner he should have. Most observers felt that John had played around with the fight and taken things far too lightly. He had perhaps been a little overconfident in his approach. Returning to his corner at the end of the bout, Dick Owens became furious with him. Overconfidence would not do. Respect must always be shown for the sport itself, and for each and every opponent. Another valuable lesson was learned that day. He never took an opponent lightly again.

John next boxed against the British Army – not all of them of course, just the one. He was selected to fight for Wales. It was a team event. It was not something out of which he expected a positive result. His opponent was older, more seasoned and a lot stronger. He duly lost the bout, but the experience that day, gained through defeat, was priceless. John fought a good, solid fight throughout, only to be beaten on points.

Then in November 1973, he received an unexpected invitation to fight against Welsh amateur champion Bryn Griffiths. The original challenger, a young boxer called Mike Pickett, had fallen ill and had had to pull out of the match. John Owens was being asked to fight instead. He was all for it. He was confident he could take the step-up. He trained well and fought even better. It paid off. He won the fight on points. He fought Bryn Griffiths again in a rematch, but this time lost on points. *C'est la vie* and *vive l'expérience*.

There were many fights in the following year. John was picked to fight for Wales again, this time against the Midlands. He won on points. At the Welsh Championships, held at Fairwater, Cardiff, John made it through to the semi-finals. He won that fight and went into the final of the Senior Championships on 4 April 1974 against a very experienced boxer from Cardiff called Maurice O'Sullivan. John outboxed O'Sullivan from the sound of the first bell to the end of the fight, but, at the end of the match, O'Sullivan was announced the winner. Dick and John were flabbergasted. They thought O'Sullivan had got away with daylight robbery. Dick complains to this day about that result.

In all fairness to O'Sullivan, he later brought the Cup over to the Owens' table. 'It should have been your Cup, John,' he said generously. O'Sullivan later went on to become Commonwealth flyweight champion.

John quickly put this ridiculous defeat behind him and was soon back to the real business of boxing. For their next fight, they travelled to West Bromwich, near Birmingham, where John had to fight a very strong and clever boxer named Ahmed Younis. It was, according to many impartial observers, John Owens' biggest test to date. He lost the match on points. It had turned out, as predicted, to be his toughest fight as well. He accepted defeat bravely and without excuse. But there was a twist at the end of the bout. Instead of being a gracious winner and wishing John well, Younis made the mistake of approaching the young Merthyr boxer and telling him that he was lucky he didn't knock him out. In all probability, John would have told him where to go and what might happen when next they met. Younis was an arrogant boxer. He wouldn't have fretted. His overconfident smile would not be erased by a threat from John Owens. What could this skeletal-looking kid from the Valleys do against him, anyway?

A few weeks later, John was again picked to fight for Wales, on this occasion against Scotland. The bout would take place on 17 May 1974. He was to box against a little-known fighter, Johnny Raeside. The kid from Merthyr felt he had a point to prove to the world that night, and he stormed in and kept on storming. Poor Johnny Raeside didn't know what had hit him. John, with a tornado of a two-fisted non-stop assault, ended the contest 30 seconds into the 2nd round. It was a great performance and one that was noticed by many experienced observers watching that evening. He was starting to cause ripples of interest amongst the boxing fraternity.

Even at this early stage in his career, John was focused. And being focused meant serious work and no time for anything much other than training. This hard graft and solid concentration was to result in a small but important victory for him. He was once again picked to fight for Wales and once again matched against his old braggart adversary, Ahmed Younis. The two young men were to fight a hard and difficult match. Both boxers gave it their all. Back and forth throughout the rounds the points gained favoured first John and then Ahmed, then back again. It see-sawed from one boxer to the other, but John seemed much stronger as the fight progressed. His opponent, though, looked as though he felt equally as confident up to the bell for the last round and thought he had won. In Younis's corner they waited confidently as the referee checked the scorecards. He drew both boxers into the centre of the ring and announced John the victor. The look of shock on Younis's face was well worth the wait. Both trainer and boxer relished the moment. Revenge had indeed been exacted in its best form. As a dish served cold!

After that fight, things were never the same again. John continued training as usual and, on the surface at least, everything seemed normal, but for whatever reason a breakthrough had been made. From this time on, John would approach the sport with a different air. He seemed to have zeal – a zest, a hunger for improvement and almost a glint in his eye – as he worked harder and harder. This must have been the time that confidence came. The time he realised he could be good at this and, with dedication and concentration, it could get better. There were two more fights in 1974. Both were for Wales. One was another against the Army in November and the other against Ireland in Dublin in December. John won both quite easily.

The Owens family had a good Christmas that year. It seemed to end a sound and reflective period in John's career. This had been a period of learning and of understanding his craft, a period of gaining valuable experience in and away from the boxing ring. There were some defeats and he had learned from them. His victories were growing and from those, too, he learned well. It felt good that Christmas. But despite the natural feelings that come from a job well done and the holiday mood, John dedicated himself to training throughout the festivities. It was a good thing he did. For very soon after the last chime of midnight on 31 December, he was to receive an invitation to box. The first call to fight in the new year was for Wales again. He would fight once more against the Midlands. John's opponent would be none other than Ahmed Younis. It was one-all between the two boxers and this little battle would decide the result of the warfare between the two young amateur boxers for ever.

Throughout the fight, John showed a superior style and displayed to one and all a huge improvement in technique and craft. He had begun to grow as a boxer. A frustrated Ahmed Younis was consistently warned for fouling and using his head. John ignored the head-butting as best he could and kept on boxing, boxing and boxing. It was the only way to defeat a man who seemed to show no regard for the rules. Younis was eventually disqualified. That particular victory for John, on that winter's night in Solihull, near Birmingham, wasn't about revenge. It was about business. And the business John was in was the business of winning.

As John became a better fighter, as he climbed the ladder of success in his trade, opponents became much more difficult to find. Victories, and the manner and style of them, meant that John was already beginning to step away from the average boxer. It didn't really trouble him too much. He never became impatient, no matter how long he had to wait for bouts to arrive. He kept up his punishing training regime regardless. But he had to wait a while to fight again. There wasn't another contest until 2 February 1975. Then he fought a young lad from Llandeilo, in west Wales. His name was Noel Evans and they were to meet at Aberdare Amateur Boxing Club. Aberdare was not far from John's home in Merthyr and the match was something of a walkover. John toyed with his inexperienced opponent, but at least it was a fight. Any ring time is better than no ring time. John stopped Noel at the beginning of the third round.

Two weeks later, John was picked again for Wales – this time against Sweden in Stockholm. When John stepped into the ring to greet his new Swedish opponent (a boxer called Laitale) and removed his dressing gown, he astonished the large home audience. Until then, John had been boxing where he had been 'known'. A small group – a club if you like – had got used to John Owens and his slight build over the years. Over time, they had developed the idea that this was just the way John was. This was how he looked. It mattered not, as long as he did the business, fought well and won his bouts. They had also given him a nickname and that nickname had begun to stick – John Owens, the Matchstick Man had arrived in Sweden.

The Swedish crowd had never seen anything like him. No one of his frame or appearance had ever fought in Sweden before and they had certainly never heard the name Matchstick Man. Almost the entire Swedish audience laughed at his expense that night. They jeered and generally had a go at the young Merthyr fighter right up to the bell. Then John began to box. And the crowd began to understand. This was no ordinary fighter. This boxer might well be special. He won the contest easily. The referee stopped the fight in the second round. The laughter had first been subdued and then stopped in its tracks.

John then began boxing as a bantamweight. His first opponent was an Englishman called Allan Smith. The fight took place at the Royal Gardens Hotel in Kensington, London, on 11 November 1975. He was once again representing his country. The team they fought against was the Metropolitan Police Amateur Boxing Club. John won on points that night and was later congratulated by none other than the heavyweight champion of Great Britain, Joe Bugner. He boxed again at bantamweight soon after and won on points against a boxer called Chris Haggerty. Within eight days of that fight, John was picked to box for Wales against the Army once more. If John thought the Swedish crowd was sceptical, he was in for some real questioning from the Army crowd in Henley when they saw the way he looked. His opponent was a Lance-Corporal Phillips. It was all John's fight that night and he won on points.

It was there, before that fight, during a routine medical, that a doctor intervened for the first time. He made known to Dick Owens that he thought the young boxer too frail to be in the ring: too frail, too thin, too precious. He felt it could be dangerous for John to fight. It was there that Dick would answer the doubting physician with the words, 'watch this'. Words he would use time and time again in the future in order to make the point both about John's physique and his boxing ability. And it was there that John Owens showed everyone how good and strong he actually was. A confused and unsure doctor had to accept the enigma of John Owens even though he could hardly believe it. Confronted with the evidence of his own eyes, he had to give in and admit that he had been wrong concerning the young boxer's ability, fitness and stamina: John was quite an amazing boxer. He said it all right, but was he convinced?

After the Welsh Amateur Championships had concluded in 1976, everyone felt it was time to move on. Time to look at John's career a little more closely. Time even perhaps for John to turn professional. He had lost the bout at the season's end to Jimmy Evans, though many impartial observers thought otherwise. Whatever the result, it didn't matter greatly in the larger scheme of things. It wasn't going to change the way the future seemed to be panning out.

John and Dick had been requested to discuss the possibilities of making the change from amateur to professional. The two of them travelled to New Tredegar, a small mining valley town close to Merthyr Tydfil, by invitation. There, they met up with boxing folk whom they thought might have the most influence on John's immediate future.

Dai Gardner, an up-and-coming, astute boxing manager in his mid-30s, with a brisk and business-like attitude and a lot of local respect, had been watching the rise of John Richard Owens for some time. He felt he had seen a champion in the making, maybe even a world champion in the making. At that time, Dai worked as a fitter for the National Gas Board, but it was as a manager of boxers that he craved success. He was an ex-boxer himself and had been no ordinary run-of-the-mill professional in his time, fighting at lightweight and welterweight. In 13 fights, he had been beaten only once. His career ended when a detached retina forced his retirement from the ring. He had retained a love of boxing, though. Dai Gardner was at New Tredegar to talk to the young Owens boy, to lay down plans for the future and make him an offer.

Boxing promoter Heddwyn Taylor also attended the meeting that night. Taylor was a perceptive and well-respected businessman throughout the Valleys and beyond, with many years of experience in the world of boxing promotions. He was there to explain to John how he would guide and help in his career from the point of view of organising his professional matches for the foreseeable future. He was also there to lend a hand in the negotiations, to explain to the boxer how the finances worked and to sort out many of the legal transactions required by law and by the British Boxing Board of Control (BBBC) before each contest. Heddwyn Taylor and Dai Gardner seemed a formidable partnership that night before John Owens, and his trainer and father.

After detailed discussions, they reached an agreement. It was confirmed that John Richard Owens would become a professional boxer. Dai Gardner would be his new manager. Heddwyn Taylor issued John with the paperwork he needed to digest in order to understand this step-up to the professional ranks. He also issued him with the forms he needed to fill in to officially complete the transaction. John's amateur career had come to an end.

7

JOHNNY OWEN

I often saw him running or training as he went up Pontsarn or up the Sanatorium Hill in Merthyr. Sometimes, you forgot how much he had to do. Then you heard he'd won something and it would make you take notice of him again. That's the loneliness of the dedicated. People never see the dark, early, rain-soaked mornings or the tramping over mountains, running through mud, or pounding a bag in the gym. We'd pass in the car and say, 'That's Johnny Owen off training again.' His life was all training and preparation, and we saw just a tiny amount of it. It doesn't take much to remember Johnny Owen, even after all these years.

Ken Bayliss, a writer from Merthyr Tydfil, 2004

It's all about respect. When you're down there, at the bottom of the pile, you get nothing but rubbish thrown at you. A man can get tired of that. His family deserve better than that. If my son, or your son or daughter or whatever, had the ability to do something special, who would we be to deny him or her the chance? What would it have to do with us anyway? Sometimes, it's not just what we do for ourselves on this planet that matters greatly; nine times out of ten, what we do affects others more than it affects us, anyway. It's what we do in relation to others that matters. What we leave behind. What we nurture. What we build. And if that means getting things started, doing something that not everyone agrees with in order to get out of the gutter, away from the tedium and the junk, then that is how it has to be. For the offspring of those who are successful, things will be better, and eventually their kids and their families will benefit big-time too. So who cares in the end? By the time it gets to grandkids, no one will even remember what they did to set it all off in the first place. It's dreams, see! When you are out of it all and at the bottom of the heap, only dreams keep you going. There is nothing else. And in boxing, especially, a damn good dream can take you a long way.

On one of the application forms that amateurs have to fill in to become professional, you are advised that you can have a pseudonym. John liked the idea, and Dick and Dai Gardner had both agreed that it would be good to have a professional fighting name. The problem was choosing it. John, the epitome of a young, loyal Welshman, and always very patriotic, suggested the name Sion Rhisart Owain – John Richard Owens, his real name, in Welsh. Eventually, he was dissuaded from adopting that particular stance. Politics and sport, especially a sport where the individual takes centre stage, simply do not mix. Being a professional boxer means the world beckons and the world is not to know the idiosyncrasies of the all-Welsh name. And who could know how the world at large would take it? Some might see it as a defiant gesture, a political stirring aimed at the neighbours next door. For all those reasons and more, Sion Rhisart Owain was shelved. In the end, John's brother, Kelvin, suggested the name Johnny Owen and John conceded. From now on, he would be called Johnny Owen, and known by everyone around him as Johnny.

On 1 September 1976, he signed the forms that made him a full professional boxer. He was now Johnny Owen, licence number 92268.

It was a proud moment and one John Owens, the up-and-coming boxer, had dreamt of for most of his young life. The moment was soon over, it didn't last long, and, with the paperwork out of the way, the task of turning Johnny Owen into a professional fighter commenced in earnest. There was much to do. It wasn't just the training or physical side of things that counted. Matches had to be secured, promotions chased up and an image had to be created. Johnny Owen well and truly became the Matchstick Man now. It was how posters would promote his image. This nickname would help him gain the attention he needed at the beginning of his career. It would help him develop his stature as a professional and then enhance his profile in the sport. Image, oddly enough, was important and his manager, the ever-watchful Dai Gardner, sensed that well. There was a long way to climb. He wasn't even at the beginning as a pro really. But it was an optimistic time, a good time. Johnny Owen began his new professional training programme at the New Tredegar Gym in the Rhymney Valley just a few miles from his home in Merthyr Tydfil.

It wasn't long after these early sessions of training that a fight was arranged for him. It was to be at Pontypool in South Wales and would be held on 30 September 1976. His opponent was George Sutton. Sutton was ranked number three in the UK. This was a huge break for the young Johnny Owen. Sutton, who attended the same amateur club as Johnny, was very strong and powerful, a skilful, courageous fighter. He would be a good test for the new young pro. Without hesitation, Johnny and Dick approved the bout. They'd fight him. It was on. They agreed it was a great opportunity. A stroke of luck had befallen them at the right time. It was exciting, too, and all three men were truly up for the challenge. Serious preparation for Johnny Owen's first professional fight began in earnest.

They felt the usual mix of tension and concern on the day of the weigh-in. They wanted to get things just right: psychologically, physically and legally. After one or two mix-ups at the weigh-in itself, Johnny was ready to fight. All had gone to plan thus far. And then the nerves jangled. The dream had begun. It was time to deliver the goods. This is when the talking stops, when hiding-places are no more. Boxing is different from all other sports. It needs finesse as well as the strong arm. It needs proper thought and attention to work, as it should. All great champions are creative thinkers. They have to be. Boxing is an art. We've all heard that said before. Each fight is different, each fight shows us something new and unique, each fight has its own drama and its own place in boxing history. Of course, boxing can be brutal and not all of its participants are artistic, but the overall idea is that the fight is settled in accordance with the rules and the structure of the sport. Johnny Owen, a great respecter of the sport's traditions, fresh from amateur ranks, was ready to stake his claim for a place in boxing history.

The hall was full the night of the contest between Sutton and Owen, and the smart money was on Sutton to stop the newcomer. After Johnny entered the ring and took off his dressing gown, exposing a full set of sparklingly clean ribs, a character in a cap and muffler shouted out, 'I thought we were having boxing! Who let the greyhound in?' The humour broke some of the tension and everybody began laughing. It helped the challenger more than it helped Sutton. Johnny relaxed a little and then he boxed well. He showed those who didn't know him or had never seen him fight his inimitable skill and style. He beat Sutton. It was a good win, a classy performance and a verdict win on points: 79–78. Dick thought Johnny had beaten him more convincingly. There were no complaints, though. The fight had gone eight rounds, each lasting two minutes. Johnny was to have only one such bout ever again at this distance. For the rest of his career, he would fight either eight-, ten-, twelve- or fifteen-round contests, each round three minutes long. The win was accepted with good grace all round. Johnny was ecstatic. The move upward had begun almost instantaneously. The decision to fight Sutton proved to be an excellent one. It put Johnny Owen right on top with the best in the land at his first contest. Johnny Owen had arrived.

Sutton had been officially heralded as the best prospect to come out of Wales since the ex-world champion featherweight boxer Howard Winstone, also from Merthyr Tydfil. Winstone turned professional in 1959 and was unbeaten in his first thirty-four contests. He picked up the European title and defended it successfully on seven occasions against fellow countrymen and those from all European shores alike. It was a title he never lost in the ring. The comparisons between Winstone and Sutton seemed a little optimistic and premature now that the newcomer Johnny Owen had beaten him well. The pundits began to sit up and take notice.

Johnny's manager was, of course, over the moon, but Dick felt the need to ground his young son and protégé in long-term planning and preparation in order to build a career and achieve consistency in shaping his world around his boxing life. One win did not make a career and Dick was cautious. Johnny had massive potential all right and he had done well, but in the rough-and-tough world of professional boxing, you're only as good as your last fight.

To be a professional, one must train hard, study the sport from all angles and eat plenty of the right foods (oh, and run and run and run). And a lot more. Keeping in shape mentally and physically was the secret. Get the balance right between contentment and fitness, and you wouldn't go far wrong. Johnny was attentive to all the advice that Dick would issue to him. And there was plenty of advice. He was lucky in that respect. One decision taken at this time was controversial, but it was not unusual in the strict, fitness-driven world of professional sport. There were to be no girlfriends for Johnny Owen. Not until he had finished his boxing career. Johnny agreed that it would not be fair to the girl or to him. If you're going to be the best, then you have to give everything. That would be impossible if a girlfriend or young wife was in tow. It was tough, but if one is to aim high, then some of the things the rest of us take for granted have to be shelved, albeit temporarily, in order to fulfil the dream. There is always something to give up. Always a price to pay. Johnny Owen accepted that dedication at this stage would see him go a long way, and to that end he gave his heart and soul. He had five weeks to train for his next contest. The match was to be against Neil McLaughlin in the Templemore Sports Complex in Londonderry, Northern Ireland, on 9 November 1976.

When the passengers on the flight to Belfast landed at the city airport on 8 November 1976, Northern Ireland was going through one of its worst times ever. Probably the worst since the Troubles began. Ironically, some people were selling poppies, the symbol of peace and resolution, as Johnny Owen passed through the airport. Armistice Day was on 11 November and certain political factions in that troubled province felt such British sentiments of remembrance were out of place in an Ireland they regarded as an independent state. Northern Ireland, at the time, was fraught with danger. Armed troops were on road checkpoints, snipers were in position and the IRA – when they weren't involved in insurrection and bombing campaigns – sometimes created violence in other ways. It was not the safest of places to go and box.

The hotel Johnny and Dick stayed at was but 100 yards away from the border with Eire. The difference could be quite overwhelming, unbelievable to some. There, in the Republic of Ireland, they largely ignored the troubles of their northern counterparts and tried to set aside all their worries and woes. Unfortunately, though almost predictably at that time in Ireland, violence was never far away from the surface. One could feel and sense it. Their personal safety remained very much at the forefront of their minds.

When they arrived at the Templemore Sports Complex, two contests had already been fought. The crowd was as boisterous as any boxing fraternity in the world. The Johnny Owen camp had been warned beforehand to expect the unexpected. It wasn't long in coming. News that a mysterious phone call had been made came through to them in the dressing-room. An anonymous caller had laid claim to a bomb, saying it had been planted in the complex and was supposed to go off any time soon. Some of the locals knew better and advised everyone to ignore the call; others were not so sure. The situation slowly filtered down to the tense soldiers guarding public safety. It would be their decision that decided the fate of the evening's boxing. They agreed to monitor the situation rather than evacuate the auditorium and allowed the sporting entertainment to proceed. Normality, if that is the word, resumed and the fights continued.

The noise of the loud and raucous crowd, along with the strange events that had already clouded the evening, added to the tension in the dressing-room as Johnny Owen prepared for the contest. He had to shrug it all off, though. This was a professional sport, and testing conditions were part of the mix. The experience would be invaluable and Johnny soon got used to the situation. So he waited, patiently. For his turn to box. Until, finally, that contest against Neil McLaughlin got under way.

McLaughlin began by backing off from the Welshman through the earlier rounds. Playing it safe. Forcing the new professional to chase him. It looked like Johnny would be running after McLaughlin all night. There was a chance, if McLaughlin's tactics continued, that the Merthyr man might not last the pace. Then, suddenly, halfway through the bout, another surprise – the lights went out. 'What der fook happened?' someone shouted as the crowd broke in angry protest. Then, just as suddenly and without explanation, the lights came on again.

The fight quickly restarted, as did the Irishman's back-pedalling tactics. Johnny chased McLaughlin all over the ring that night, pinning him on the ropes throughout the contest. When the final bell rang, the referee gave the result as a draw. It was what they call in boxing circles, a 'home-town decision' (one that favours the local boxer). It happens quite often. Not as often, one might add, as some grumbling points-losers of the ring have consistently made out, but it happens just the same. Johnny Owen should have won. He hadn't. But he hadn't lost either. That was the main thing. The judges didn't have enough ammunition to give the fight to McLaughlin. The Owen camp were naturally disappointed, but after the strange events of the night they were not downhearted. They left the ring in good humour. They could at least return home to Wales with everything intact (thank God).

Johnny's next contest was for Eddie Thomas Promotions at the Rhondda Sports Centre in Tonypandy. The match was to be held on 23 November 1976. His opponent this time was to be Ian Murray from Manchester. It was a much easier fight for Johnny and he outgunned Murray, putting his opponent on the canvas twice. The referee had little choice but to stop the contest in the seventh round.

And so came Christmas 1976. With three professional wins under his belt, Johnny Owen could afford to relax a little and take things easy. Everything seemed to be going well. He appeared to be heading in the right direction. The holiday should have been a time for reflection, but, in truth, the holiday made little difference to Johnny Owen's normal hard-working life. The roadwork and training didn't switch off just because of the holidays. Johnny celebrated his 21st birthday on 7 January 1977 with more training.

It was a good thing he continued to train because Dai Gardner informed him soon after the new year had crawled in that he was to fight for Midlands promoter Dave Roden at a West Bromwich Gala on 28 January. Johnny was to fight his old rival Neil McLaughlin of Northern Ireland again. It would be his first professional return bout. This time, the fight would be less socially traumatic and easier for everyone concerned. Johnny won it well. It was a relatively stress-free, clean-and-tidy win. He had worked out his opponent at their first meeting. He'd done his homework and it had reaped rewards. The scorecard ended up 80–76, Johnny beating McLaughlin on points.

One of the oddest things of all, in relation to this time of success for Johnny Owen, was that whilst he was climbing first the amateur and then the professional ranks in the boxing world, he was also holding down a full-time job. This anomaly is something today's modern sportsmen and women rarely have to deal with. Professional sport today is full-on. You go for it – sponsorship, television, the lot. It wasn't like that back then. The money was not in sport as a whole as it is today. You sometimes had to work and play in order to develop a career. So, since the day he'd left school, Johnny Owen had been working at a local factory in Abercanaid, a small village a few miles south of Merthyr Tydfil. The Suko nut and bolt factory had employed Johnny as a young man of 16. He was a good worker and, over the years, had risen from fitter to charge hand. He had always been treated well by his bosses. The job had given him an income and had not upset either his fight preparations or his training routine. Frank Martin, a lovely man and a great Johnny Owen supporter, was the foreman and ultimately Johnny's boss.

'We knew well enough the boxer's need to train hard,' said Martin. 'We wanted to support Johnny all we could and, though we were never easy on him, that is to say we would not promote inequality in the workplace, we did look after him.' Frank Martin came up with an innovative idea for the boxer at the time, and offered Johnny Owen and his trainer a very unusual proposal.

Martin took them both to the old canal that used to ferry the iron and coal from Merthyr Tydfil to Cardiff in the early days of the industrial age. On a busy day, many, many years before they stood looking at it, the canal would have been noisy and abuzz with activity. When the railways took over the freight business, they closed the canal. It was now quiet and deserted. An old cottage sitting between the broken-down, derelict Gethin Colliery in Abercanaid and the canal itself was owned by a friend of Frank Martin's called Darren Hill. Martin asked Johnny if he wanted to try his hand at chopping down a few trees around the property. Would it help his training, perhaps? The pine trees were not great in number – it was not exactly a forest – but it certainly was a fair-sized wood. It was a fantastic idea and just what was needed at this time in Johnny's professional career. The young boxer was pleased. This would be an ideal place for him to build up much-needed strength.

Boxing promoter Heddwyn Taylor approached Dai Gardner with the idea of securing a return match between Johnny Owen and George Sutton, but this time for the prestigious Welsh title. This was big-time promotion indeed and a title fight to boot. But there were problems. The Welsh Area Boxing Council refused to recognise the bid. They intimated that Johnny Owen was too inexperienced (even though he'd beaten Sutton previously in a non-title bout!). Arguments went on and on, as Dai Gardner and Heddwyn Taylor tried to reverse the Area Council's decision and secure the bout. But the impetus of the arguments put forward by them flew out of the window when Eddie Thomas Promotions announced yet another fight promotion between Johnny Owen and Neil McLaughlin.

Moans of 'Not again!' rang around the valley. And it wasn't just the moans of the fans. The Johnny Owen camp was not too pleased, either. Still, it was a fight. And it was set to take place at Rhydycar Centre in Merthyr Tydfil on 15 February 1977. Johnny won again. Neil McLaughlin just couldn't get the better of the Welshman. The bout served little purpose other than to augment the argument for the Sutton title fight to go ahead. It built up his CV under the heading 'Experience', although it wasn't a very good contest.

Then, from out of the blue, came news from the Welsh Area Boxing Council. They had changed their minds having reconsidered the decision concerning the possibilities of a contest between Johnny Owen and George Sutton. The title fight was on. It was down to the original promoter, Heddwyn Taylor, to develop and promote the fight. He did so with relish and Johnny Owen's first Championship title bout took place at Ebbw Vale Leisure Centre on 29 March 1977.

Despite his lack of ring experience, Johnny entered the arena with a confidence and assurance that meant business. He was here to take his chance and grab the opportunity presented to him. He was fighting now at a level he'd been preparing for all his boxing life. It was a dream come true. Johnny knew he had the stuff of champions running through his veins, even if no one else could see it yet (least of all those at the Welsh Council). Now, he had the chance to prove it. This self-assurance was soon justified. A very sporting, hard-fought and exciting contest took place. It was touch-and-go between champion and challenger throughout the earlier rounds, but Johnny's stamina began to tell towards the end of the fight. When the judges met, they decided that Johnny Owen had done enough to deserve a win. It had seemed a lot easier to judge for those sitting in the audience than it had been to those deciding the fate of the bout. Most saw clearly that Johnny had been the superior of the two boxers that night. Whatever the ins and outs of the decision, the title of Welsh champion was given to the Merthyr Tydfil boxer. Johnny had won the fight on points: 99–97. Johnny Owen was Welsh bantamweight champion.

The hard training and dedication had paid off. Johnny Owen was Welsh champ! Everyone that had anything to do with his winning the title was jubilant. At the end of the fight, when he had calmed down slightly, everything seemed the same, but it wasn't and would never be the same again. Everything was different. The world had changed for ever for the new Welsh champion. There was no going back now. The genie was out of the bottle. The media in Wales all of a sudden woke up to the fact that they had a new champion on their hands and he just might be something special. They began to develop a keen, urgent interest in this new fighting character from Merthyr Tydfil. The world was slowly coming to realise that Johnny Owen, the relatively new bantamweight boxing professional from the Welsh Valleys, was perhaps world class. It was time for the Welsh media to come on board. Time to cash in on the story that would now surely follow. Time to follow the rise of the new Welsh champion as he strove for bigger and better things. Time to climb aboard the dream.

About eight o'clock on the morning after that first Championship fight, the television and newspaper journalists were knocking on the door of Mr and Mrs Richard Owens of Bryn Padell, Gellideg in Merthyr Tydfil. Pandemonium had broken loose. Television cameras, reporters and those there merely to wish Johnny well were all gathered to greet the new Welsh champion on that mad, mad morning.

Everyone wanted to talk to the young man who had seemingly come from nowhere to become a champion. The boy that they had seen running everywhere, but had never really taken much notice of, was now recognised. The same young man who spent his afternoons chopping down trees was now known to everyone as the Welsh champion. As is often the case with these things, Johnny Owen had not just arrived out of the blue; he was no overnight success. He had worked hard over many years for everything and had genuinely earned this title. He knew, as did those around him, that his work had barely begun. This was the first step on the road to the top. It was not the end of the journey, it was just the end of the beginning.

8

MEXICAN MONDAY

Set some 2,400 metres above sea level, in its shallow mountain bowl and crammed with over 20 million people (from fewer than 5 million in 1960), Mexico City is one of the world's most densely populated urban areas. It is said to receive 1,000 immigrants each day from the rest of the country. At times frustrating, the longer you spend in the city the more rewarding it can become, with unstructured wandering throwing up all sorts of surprises. After a few days, you will be able to get around the main sights and soak up a good deal of the vibrant atmosphere. The capital is nowhere near as intimidating as you might expect. Nonetheless, you may still prefer to take in the city a couple of days at a time, taking off in between to the smaller neighbouring colonial cities to recharge. You'll also find Mexico City easier still if you acclimatise to the country first. If at all possible, try not to spend too long there when you first arrive.

The Mexican morning sun was dying to get into the room. I knew it was out there, high above the city; I sensed that it blazed in glory even without seeing it for myself. I felt its presence as it oozed through every gap in the curtain-covered, four-star-hotel bedroom window. Having just arrived from a harsh, dark European winter, I was very much looking forward to drawing the drapes and letting the light in. I lay there for a second wondering if I'd feel any jet lag. Would I suffer for the journey across the globe? I was not usually very good at these transatlantic voyages. Still, one has to accept that generally you do have to pay your dues. I have learned that much. Whatever it is that gains you, there is a payback: something else will sneak up and pain you. Never celebrate a winning bet, it might be your last. The next ten wagers might well be lessons in 'character building'. And we all need those, don't we?

I got up. Gingerly, I stepped across the room. My body was tired all right, but not so much as I'd really notice. I'd been worse. Strangely enough, I felt good. Optimism began to rear its ugly head (always a bad sign, this). I opened the curtains and at last let the sunshine in (whilst singing the song of the same title). After recovering my sight, it was time to recover my body and get ready for our 'breakfast meeting'. I prepared myself for the enamel day ahead, shaving and whistling 'Waterloo Sunset' by The Kinks. Gradually, I resumed correspondence with the reasons for my being here and wondered why I was so cheerful. We Irish-Welsh Celts are not known for morning good humour. I recalled the previous evening.

Getting through the airport hadn't been as bad as I thought it might have been. Dylan, Dick and I had stuck together and, although the queues were long and slow, there were no real problems to bar our entry into the sovereign state of Mexico. Some of the officials, mind you, looked like they'd just stepped off the set of a Clint Eastwood Spaghetti Western, which was rather interesting. I was really hoping one of them would call out '*Gringo*!' to me at some stage. It would have been a wonderful experience to hear the accent used properly, Hollywood-style, like it ought to be. It would have made my day. Alas, it never happened.

I was the first through Customs and the first out on Mexican soil. Dick and Dylan joined me soon after. Once we were free from the intrusions and legal machinations of the system, we set off first to get some Mexican money and then to organise a taxi to drive us across the city to our hotel.

As far as I could see, the trick was now to try to avoid finding a taxi driver whose sole intention was to give us a sight-seeing tour of Mexico City in the dark. Without being asked. And then charge us $200 for the absolute pleasure of doing so. I felt it best to point out to my travelling companions that it would perhaps be wise to seek advice regarding taxis. A friend of a friend knew an occasion in Colombia where a taxi driver had picked up a fare and taken the poor soul to a desert. After a brief and hopeless scuffle, the taxi driver rendered the fare unconscious. The said taxi driver then relieved the passenger of all worldly goods, leaving the comatose body for the wildlife to dispose of. The cab driver got caught in the end and Colombian justice ran its course (he's probably prime minister now!). But that's not the point.

Dylan quite rightly jumped on another point. Colombia was quite a long way from Mexico. I agreed, but added that perhaps we should allow caution to rule, at least during these early exchanges in this strange and warm foreign land. We got some money and found a taxi, and for Mexico City we embarked. I still nurtured the hope of seeing a bank held up by unshaven, podgy Mexican bandits with cheroots sticking out of their mouths and cartridge bandoliers strapped diagonally across their chests. They'd spit at us and say, 'Geeeve us you are munnee yew peece of sheeet!' But Mexico City, late on this Sunday night, was black, seemingly bleak and strangely empty. They'd had rain. The streets shone like Welsh streets do in early-morning winter. Dick and I sat together in the back seat of the cab and nervously chatted about this and that, and soon we pulled up at the hotel entrance. It looked a rather decent place.

The breakfast buffet was bountiful. After helping myself to some eggs, toast, cereal and coffee, I scanned the large, very busy dining room. Dick Owens was sitting alone at a table laid for six beneath a window through which could be seen the top of the city. I headed across to join him. Dylan arrived soon after and was quickly followed by the film's producer Ynyr Williams, a youngish, ambitious television and film producer with much experience, and an unusual and decent lack of cynicism (for the TV business, that is). He would not just produce this film, but double up on sound recording too.

That morning, a very tired and troubled Ynyr and our cameraman for the week, one Huw Talfryn-Walters, a friendly and most obliging character, sat and recalled their journey to Mexico via New York. Apparently, all had gone relatively well until they arrived in Mexico City itself. Then things had soured somewhat on their way to the hotel. They gave us a hair-raising tale of running out of petrol in their hired van in the middle of no-man's-land downtown Mexico City with all the equipment and money on board at three o'clock in the morning. They were lucky to be alive. Little wonder they looked so worn out. After they were done, we three exchanged the tame tale of our journey. Ynyr had prepared us all a sort of 'diary for the week ahead' and there would be no straying from the plan. The handout made for very interesting reading.

The film documentary we had all been sent here to work on was essentially about Dick Owens' journey from Merthyr Tydfil to Mexico City to meet and confront the ex-bantamweight champion of the world, Lupe Pintor. More than 20 years had elapsed since Pintor had fought Johnny Owen in Los Angeles for the Bantamweight World Championship. Pintor had won the fight. Dick had watched from his son's corner that night. The meeting between the two men had been planned, but not choreographed. No one in this little-scripted outing, least of all the central protagonists – Dick Owens and Lupe Pintor – had any idea as to what was going to happen when the meeting eventually took place. It was how both men wished it to be. The breakfast chatter that morning quickly moved on to the possibilities this encounter might throw up. The conversation was excited, and full of creative ideas and anticipated potential.

Although he was here and along for the filming ride with us, Dick was not really a part of it all. At least, not quite like we were. We were outsiders doing a job, getting copy onto film. He had many other tiring thoughts to concern him, many personal memories to come to terms with before he returned to Merthyr Tydfil in seven days' time. I felt he would have little rest this week. It was going to be very different for him. We had plenty to keep us busy and I personally had lots of research to commit to paper, so we would be all right. He would be hanging about, perhaps doing a little acting and posing for camera, and being the interviewee. These were not tasks most people would enjoy at any time, let alone with the added burdens Dick carried. We all agreed that we would take Dick Owens' feelings into account whenever we could and always try to remember to understand how and why things were different for him in Mexico from what they were for us.

That day, though, two days before the meeting with Lupe Pintor, neither he nor I would be needed on the film set. The production team would be setting everything up; it was a day of reconnaissance. My job, on this bright and warm, stunning spring Monday in Mexico was to look after Dick Owens and prepare background for the interviews that were to follow later in the week. Conveniently, as we were winding up breakfast, the BBC translator (Mexican Spanish to English, no problem!), Jorge Eduardo Sanchez no less, arrived, along with our van driver/personal minder for the week, a big, burly, fierce-looking man called Raul. They would become close to us as the project developed and began to take shape. Both would become a genuine part of the team. After we'd exchanged brief farewells with the rest of the group, Dick and I were left alone. We arranged to take a walk around the city, at least the hotel area, after a short but much-needed mid-morning siesta, and then return to a quiet part of the hotel dining room for lunch and the main business of the day: the first interview on this trip to discuss Johnny Owen, past, present and future.

We walked for what seemed like miles, and probably was. The madness that is Mexico City was quite overwhelming, but extremely enlightening. The road outside our hotel was the main road around the city centre. There were eight lanes of traffic on either side, some going south, some north. From the time Dick and I left the hotel to the time we returned a couple of hours later, those sixteen lanes were never quiet. Never once were they devoid of traffic. It was continuous traffic, too, and the cars and taxis and vans and buses and lorries and campers that passed through were rarely new or eco-friendly. Mexico was a carbon-dioxide death trap. It seemed that if the cars didn't get you, then the gas would. Dick summed it up perfectly and continued to use the same word all week, each occasion he found himself walking out in this transportation mess. He'd first stand his ground, look north and south, then shake his head, tut-tutting in disbelief. 'Uncanny,' he'd mutter. 'Uncanny.' And he was absolutely right. It was uncanny. It was also unbelievable, unhealthy, unfamiliar and unsustainable.

On that first foray into Mexico City, we mainly walked along the backstreets behind the hotel. It was astonishing to us how quiet it all was back there. In contrast to the main street, this was heaven. We visited shops and cafés, a supermarket and a kind of unfinished shopping mall some two miles or so away from our base. We tried to keep off the main roads as much as we could and were both pleasantly surprised by most of our discoveries. Many of the stores were clean, friendly and economically attractive, and most held a varied and bountiful supply of all kinds of interesting and valuable merchandise. It was better than home in many respects. But the walk was not really what it was all about. None of any of this was. We were playing around the edges.

Dick Owens was here to help with a film. I was here to talk to him, interview him and find out more than I already knew in preparation for the documentary and the book I had now embarked upon. I began the inevitable questioning during that walk around the hotel's vicinity. The questions were never meant to be probing or inventive, or of a truth-seeking exposé type. This was Dick's story and, as far as everyone was concerned, he could tell it as he wished.

I asked Dick about Johnny Owen's legacy. What did he think it was? How did he think Johnny would be remembered? How did he and his wife Edith feel about it all now, after the passing of time? Dick responded at length. He believed that Johnny's legacy, not only as a boxer but also as a unique human being, must be preserved. Johnny had shown how hard work, determination and dedication when added to talent and the ability to dream big could work in anyone's favour anywhere. The lessons of Johnny's life must be positive and well learned by the young people that now follow him in the world of boxing. If that were to happen, then a certain value could be placed upon Johnny's life, a value beyond even the priceless value his family had always placed on him. I understood what he was trying to say and urged him to continue. He proceeded to do so with little prompting.

He and Edith had lost their son at a very young age. They were, and still are, heartbroken by the tragic turn of events that took Johnny away from them. The years for both of them had not diminished their son's memory in any way whatsoever. The events are as painful now as then and that is how it always will be, he said. His legacy to them would be one of a loving son. He had shown them love and cared for them. What more was there to ask of a child? They were thankful for having been given Johnny Owen in the first place.

I began to think a lot more deeply about all of this myself. For a father to lose a son must be the most difficult thing in the world to accept. In Dick Owens' situation, uniquely and more tragically so. I wondered how he'd felt that night in Los Angeles just before the last bell in Johnny Owen's life rang out. Was he still full of hope for the title then? Did he still feel confident they could win?

In the height of battle, mistakes are often made. It is where the real test of a human being often lies. It is at crisis point that we show to all around us who we really are. They were at crisis point in the heat of awesome battle that night in Los Angeles, and in full public gaze. Many have written that what happened at that crisis point was a mistake, that errors were made, that the fight should have been stopped. Courage was needed at crisis point that night and it was unmistakably shown, but was it the right kind of courage? There were criticisms all right. These critiques were written after the event, in hindsight. None can really get to the reality of it all. No one actually blamed anyone for anything that took place that night at the fight, nor should they, but many questioned the decisions that were made. To me, they were the correct ones, of that there can be no doubt, because they were made as they should have been made – on merit.

Some blamed boxing for what happened to Johnny Owen, but there was another way of looking at the whole thing, and Dick quickly recognised and understood the point. He immediately came up with a proposal that resonated. Yes, Johnny had died young, but boxing could not be blamed. Life was like that. You win some, you lose some. In boxing, as in life, this is also the case. The family and friends of Johnny Owen were fortunate indeed to have had him as son, brother and companion for his lifetime. And that is what it was, no more and no less. It was his lifetime. What the good Lord allocated him.

I paused there, sensing we needed a break. We walked a while in silence through the back roads of Mexico City, beyond our hotel complex. We bought some bottled water. The day had become very hot and humid, promising a thunderstorm. We strolled nonchalantly toward that crazy main 16-lane road of mindless traffic and impossible crossings, and then on to the hotel. We strolled in silence. As soon as we arrived at the main road, Dick pulled up, took a swig of water, looked first north, then south, and tut-tutted. 'Uncanny,' he mumbled at the traffic. 'Uncanny.' And it was.

9

BOXING IS A SERIOUS BUSINESS

'Where are we going?'
'To the top, Johnny!'
'To the top? To the top of what?'
'To the toppermost of the poppermost!'

The Beatles, in a beat-up van on
their way from Liverpool to London, 1962

Winning the Welsh title had left the door slightly ajar for Johnny to make a challenge for the British title. The big guns of boxing were within his sights and the Owen camp was very aware of it. They talked openly about the possibility of a forthcoming contest with Paddy Maguire, the supremely talented bantamweight champion of Great Britain. It wouldn't be easy. It wouldn't even be easy to get there, let alone to fight him, but at least there was the potential to make a bid. It was up to the new Welsh champion to kick that door in and introduce himself. The work would start right away. A lot of blood, sweat and tears lay ahead.

The new champion of Wales, although elated, was also pragmatic and well aware of the task at hand. He'd won his first Championship title bout, but knew instinctively that getting to the top was one thing – staying there, maintaining the momentum to move ever upward and forward, was quite another. But he was inspired by his Welsh title win and understood the price that had to be paid for continuing success. He would have to train harder than he had ever done before and run forever in his roadwork to effect a genuine and serious challenge to Maguire. He would also need a fight or two under his belt at this new higher level to let Maguire see that he was the only credible challenger. That would take time. Johnny Owen had no problem with that. He had plenty of time. And plenty of patience, too. Paying the price of success was not something that bothered him greatly. Johnny was free of worry. No one would need to be concerned about his attitude or application. He was a manager's and trainer's dream.

In April 1977, promoter Les Roberts acquired the rights to the British bantamweight title fight and the services of the champion, Paddy Maguire. He was looking for a worthy challenger and Johnny Owen was amongst those being touted around. A path to the top was opening up for the young boxer. If he could get to a point where he could become undisputed challenger, then his big chance would almost certainly arrive sooner rather than later. The reigning champ was casting his eye around the contenders, looking for a new challenge. Johnny Owen had arrived on the scene at an opportune time. The fates were conspiring in his favour.

Johnny's next opponent was, on paper at least, the only man to stand in the way of a title shot against Maguire. His name was Johnny Kellie, a strong, tough fighter and champion of Scotland. At first, the talk was of a fight between Owen and Kellie being some kind of eliminator. The winner to get a crack at Paddy Maguire. It wasn't official, but both boxers went into it believing that if they won the bout, they would then fight for the British title. The fight between them was to be held at the Albany Hotel, Glasgow, on 25 April 1977.

Johnny weighed in for the fight at 114½ lb   (8 st. 2½ lb). The officials put it down as 115 lb. This came as a relief to Dick, who had a feeling that Johnny might have weighed in a little too light. He had thought they might have to withdraw. A bantamweight boxer's weight falls between 112 lb (8 st. plus) and 118 lb (8 st. 6 lb) so they were clearly all right, on that score at least. The rest of the day passed quickly and easily, and before they knew it, the fight was under way with all weigh-in worries consigned to history.

Johnny started off well. He put all the pressure on Kellie and never let up. Kellie, though, began holding as a means of defence. This was a nuisance more than a problem, so when Johnny came back to the corner it was Dai Gardner who gave the advice. He told his young charge should Kellie hold him again, he should dispose of him by throwing him off. Johnny followed these instructions to the letter, and with great gusto and enthusiasm. The next time Kellie held onto Johnny, he literally threw the Scot to the canvas. This upset and annoyed referee Wally Thom, who then gave Johnny a stern lecture about pushing his opponent. He ticked him off for breaking the rules. Johnny was furious because Kellie had not been spoken to as well. After all, he had been the one holding him in the first place. That was the original offence. He felt extremely hard done by. More problems with the rules occurred later in the fight when Johnny lost his gumshield. The referee was not in a very generous mood towards the Merthyr man and was having none of it. He made Johnny Owen box without it. This was turning into 'one of those fights': a fight that was awkward to win and would be remembered for the wrong reasons. Johnny couldn't believe such a decision. It was blatantly unfair.

The judgement to box on without the gumshield made Johnny Owen as mad as hell. He didn't like the referee's unfair decision one bit and tore into Kellie. In a way, the referee helped Johnny get through the fight. The opponent from Scotland was soon taking a real beating and was quickly knocked to the canvas twice. There was nowhere for Kellie to hide. He was a beaten man. The referee stopped the contest in the seventh round. It was a lesson not just to Johnny but to Dick as well. 'I turned professional after that,' Dick said afterwards. There would be no more lost gumshields in Johnny Owen's corner from then on.

Whatever the mistakes of that night, it was a good win. The bandwagon rolled on and Johnny was being noticed more and more by the nation's media and boxing promoters alike. The love affair between the young bantamweight and the British press had begun.

That aside, Johnny could now set his sights on fighting for the British title. They celebrated the win over Kellie in style with a little champagne, and a bag of fish and chips! The young champion stuck steadfastly to his usual orange juice, of course.

Soon after people had settled into the idea of Johnny Owen being Welsh champion, and got used to the fact that he was fast becoming the only credible and genuine challenger to Paddy Maguire, word came of a possible promotion offer. It was Dai Gardner who arrived with the news. Unfortunately, it wasn't to be Paddy Maguire, and so not a tilt at the British title; the offer that came in was for Johnny to fight at the Midland Social Club in Solihull. It was short notice. They wanted the match to take place three days later, on the Monday. Should he agree, the boxer he would be booked to fight was none other than his old adversary, George Sutton. Johnny's reply was yes. The fight was quickly agreed between the two men. Johnny and Dick began the final preparations immediately.

The fight itself turned out to be a really good contest. Just what the Welsh champion needed and not an easy workout, as some predicted it might be. It would be memorable for one incident – an event which would turn into a useful lesson for Johnny Owen. Something he would have to accept and deal with, and always remember.

In one of the earlier rounds, Johnny got careless. George Sutton clipped him on the jaw. Johnny's legs wobbled, and he looked dazed and surprised at the result of George's punch, not quite believing the power. He had fought Sutton before. He had never displayed that kind of punch, nor was he known for it. George had obviously learned a lot about Johnny's technique since the last time the two fighters met. For a moment, George himself looked as surprised as his rocky opponent, but he was too slow to capitalise on it. The effects of the blow lasted but a few seconds. Johnny shook off the attack and went after George once again, adhering to the old maxim 'the best form of defence is attack'. George had had his chance. He had not taken the advantage. Johnny went on to win the eight-round bout on points. The lesson he learned was obvious: in any fight, at any stage, in any one split-second, you are liable to get caught by your opponent's attack or counter-attack. One punch is all it takes. You cannot afford to relax for one second. Once the bell has sounded, you must at all times be mentally and physically aware. Johnny had won the bout, but he had received a scare in so doing.

After this victory, the offer of a chance to fight Paddy Maguire was placed firmly on the table. It had taken its time. After all, the so-called eliminator against John Kellie had long since passed and nothing had come of that. Still, the chance was here now and for that they were grateful. The contest to decide who was to be the champion bantamweight boxer of Great Britain (it was always called Great Britain back then, not the UK or the United Kingdom) and Northern Ireland was to be held at the National Sporting Club in London. Initially, Dai Gardner had optimistically hoped that the fight would go ahead at nearby Ebbw Vale. Dai had lobbied long and hard to have the bout fought in Wales. It would have gained Johnny a much-needed and valuable local fan support and cut out travelling time, along with the other distractions associated with London and the Club. This time they were unlucky.

Johnny had two months to prepare for the biggest fight of his young life. He must have been wondering back then how far all this would take him. It may even have begun to seem easy for him. Many new, young athletes come into sports and find the initial entry easy. They are at that period where fear hasn't yet become a factor in their performance, the time when they have nothing to lose and everything to gain. That kind of sportsperson is supremely dangerous to those already established. They have arrived to take over the sport, to move it on. They very often have no respect for reputations. When Lester Piggott beat Sir Gordon Richards for the first time and secured space for his mount as he passed the great jockey, he famously said, 'Move over, Granddad!' In the modern era, too, witness Boris Becker in tennis, Muhammad Ali in boxing, Ian Botham in cricket and George Best in football. All made a huge initial impact on their respective sports. All were blessed with supreme natural talent and were fearless in their early approaches. Johnny Owen fell into this category on the evidence he had presented thus far. With two months' training time left before the fight of his life, he began working in deadly earnest.

Dai Gardner had four to five boxers intermittently sparring with Johnny during the build-up to the fight. Johnny was also training fifteen rounds three or four times a week. His regime was relentless. It always had been, but this time it was supremely so. A would-be champion needs to be prepared and focused properly before any major fight. Nothing must be left to chance. All things are taken care of in training. You are at your peak once in this game – the minute you step into that ring. If you're not, you're doomed.

Johnny ran and ran and ran. His stamina levels increased beyond expectation. The running and the ringwork combined seemed to be doing it for him. All was going well. Roll on fight night. He was becoming more and more hopeful as each day passed by.

On top of the sparring and the fifteen rounds he endured three or four times a week, along with all the roadwork and the running, Johnny was once again cutting down the trees as part of his strict training regimen. This was the ultimate in bodybuilding for him and he enjoyed it immensely, too. He became so taken up by the task that he sometimes kept on going. It enveloped him. There was a strange hypnotic quality about taking down one tree after another. It felt good and it created for him a feeling of supreme fitness. To an outsider, it must have looked crazy, this young man incessantly chopping down tree after tree, but to Johnny it was a great way to train, to build up the body and concentrate the mind. Without anyone around telling him to stop and move on, Johnny became machine-like in his work. One day, someone from a nearby field snapped him out of his concentrated efforts. He saw Johnny chopping down a certain batch of trees that he shouldn't have been anywhere near. 'Bloody hell!' the man shouted over. 'Don't chop down any of those trees, there's a preservation order on them. You'll land up in jail!' Johnny had to curb his enthusiasm. He'd strayed off limits without realising it. He had to look elsewhere for his next set of victims.

Training days passed swiftly and without a hitch. With the training over, they travelled to London from Wales on the Monday in preparation for the contest which was to be held on the Tuesday, 29

November 1977. The night before the bout they stayed at the Regent Hotel. It was a relaxing night for Johnny. His trainer gave him a pre-fight massage and the challenger went to bed early. The following day at the weigh-in, everything went smoothly.

It must have been some night for Johnny. One wonders if he slept at all. Nothing much seemed to faze the young man, so he probably slept like a log. He had come such a long way. Here he was sleeping in his room at the Regent, awaiting yet another appointment with fate, ticking off yet another episode in his progress to the top.

As the pre-fight fanfare commenced, Johnny entered the arena with his cornermen. The tables were set out after dinner and the chandeliers, the silence, the black ties and dinner jackets all helped to create an atmosphere of intimidation. The National Sporting Club was steeped in tradition: a men-only club (hard to believe these days, but it was), it always promoted its fights behind closed doors, where applause was only allowed between rounds. One of the principal philosophies associated with the venue was this idea of intimidation. The concept was to create an aura that would make challengers and newcomers nervous, make them feel that fighting in this place would be different, that it was a special place to box and the match would be a special test of their abilities. There was a certain kind of logic attached to the theory of intimidation at the Club, but that theory was lost on the young man from Wales. It did not bother Johnny Owen one bit to be fighting there. He couldn't give a hoot about the place or its doctrine or Paddy Maguire, the champion (although he respected Maguire's boxing abilities). Johnny Owen was there to do a job. He was totally unfazed by the importance of the fight or the venue.

All thoughts of outside tactics were quickly dispelled as the fight itself got under way. Johnny dominated from the beginning, left jabs flowing. Paddy Maguire was a strong champion, a very powerful, experienced man, and crafty with it, but he seemed to have little defence against Johnny's long reach and, when he did get close, the Merthyr man was too alert to be caught. Still, the opening rounds were about even, though the wind was very much blowing in

Owen's direction. The champ was warned a few times for use of the head and Johnny took a lot of low blows, but the challenger gradually got on top of his opponent with his usual skill and tenacity as the two boxers settled into a fighting rhythm, relentlessly pursuing the champion with awesome stamina and fitness. Round after round, Maguire could find no escape from the machine that Johnny Owen was fast becoming.

Johnny was ahead by the seventh on most people's scorecards and in the eighth had Maguire in all sorts of trouble. The champion managed to see out the round. Maguire rallied in the ninth and got back into contention, but Johnny finished his chances when he cut him badly in the tenth round. There was no way back for Paddy Maguire from there. The referee, Sid Nathan, stopped the fight 1 minute and 24 seconds into the 11th round with blood streaming from Maguire's cut eye. Johnny Owen had sent the champion of Great Britain into well-earned retirement with a ruthless display of skill and stamina. The new champion had never looked like losing and didn't come across to anyone at the National Sporting Club that night as a boxer who had boxed only nine times as a professional to date. It was an amazing feat.

Johnny Owen had beaten Paddy Maguire. He had won the British Bantamweight Championship. He was champion of Great Britain. He had become the first Welsh bantamweight champion of Great Britain since Bill Beynon in 1913. They couldn't believe it. No one knew what to do. So they jumped up and down and sang. Johnny received the winner's belt that night from the Duke of Gloucester. Paddy Maguire immediately announced his retirement from the ring. Sir Gordon Richards looked down from above and nodded sagely.

As they put the belt around Johnny's waist, everyone who had been part of the story, part of the planning and the training, and even the supporting, jumped into the ring with him. It was beautiful anarchy, beautiful Welsh anarchy for a while, and so ironic that it should take place at the National Sporting Club. Dick Owens was the only absentee from the ring celebrations. He stood watching from the sidelines, in the shadows. It was reported that he had tears running down his cheeks. When asked how he felt, he could say nothing other than, 'That's my son, my son.'

Johnny Owen had made it. A path to greatness and boxing immortality had opened up before him.

10

THE CHAMP

A round consists of only three minutes. Then the men retire to their corners and sit down, lean their heads back against a post, and gasp and pant like fish while they are fanned. One fans with a tablecloth, another rubs the legs and sponges off the face and shoulders, and blows sprays of water in the fighter's face from his own mouth. Only one minute is allowed for this, then time is called and they jump up and go to fighting again. It is absorbingly interesting.

The hotel was stirring for breakfast. A barrage of reporters and photographers were outside waiting. The press had caught up with the champion. A still-sleepy Johnny Owen made his way through the splendid hotel to greet them. When he got outside, he stood in professional, image-making mode before the camera flashes, posing for a few fans and curious passers-by, proudly showing off his newly won Lonsdale belt, raising it high in the old tradition of the winner. The press ordeal over, he returned to the dining room where he ate a substantial and well-earned breakfast. The new champ was in good spirits. He was learning the media ropes fast too. Nothing much seemed to faze him.

Everyone who had been involved with the previous evening's

successful challenge was at that breakfast table with him. Talking across it, ten to the dozen, they were elated beyond their wildest dreams. They dissected the fight. They argued over the best points, the worst points, the referee, the crowd, everything they could think of until gradually they agreed it was the best fight they had ever seen. It was glorious pandemonium. They were caught up in the magnificent reality of it all. Johnny Owen was a double champ: champion of Wales and Great Britain. It was a unique achievement. And this after only nine professional fights!

They arrived back in Merthyr Tydfil at around 3.30 p.m. that same day, a little tired but not too shaken up. They had to first return their hired car. The owner of the car-hire firm, Gary Thomas, gave the Owen camp their first taste of fame. He invited them all into his office and opened a bottle of champagne in Johnny's honour. Appropriately, they would toast the new champ for the first time in his home town with champagne. Aneurin Bevan, the left-wing firebrand Labour leader and founder of the National Health Service, with a long and deep association with Merthyr Tydfil and its people, would have been proud. 'Why cannot a miner drink champagne?' he once asked when arguing for the cause of freedom and opportunity for workers. One or two glasses of champagne later and the 'workers' were in the mood for celebrating yet again. And they did. Except for Johnny, who drank orange juice. Johnny Owen rarely took anything alcoholic.

Another party had been arranged that night at the New Inn in Tredegar, and yet another at Gary Thomas's nightclub (the same Gary Thomas who owned the car-hire firm), the Brandy Bridge. There, at the club, the Mayor of Merthyr Tydfil was to launch a new talking book for the blind. She would also meet the new bantamweight champion of Great Britain and Wales, Johnny Owen. The Mayor wasn't a keen fight fan, though, and failed to recognise the frail, shy-looking man standing next to her. 'Who are you, and what have you done?' she asked. Straight to the point, down to earth, that's how they are in Merthyr Tydfil. It was pointed out that this unassuming young man was in fact none other than Johnny Owen. She was extremely embarrassed by her obvious gaffe. She didn't made that mistake

THE CHAMP

again.

As a way of making up for this minor slight upon Merthyr's newly discovered rising sports star, she invited him to the Mayor's Parlour the following morning, an honour indeed. There, she posed for photographs with Johnny Owen. Someone in the small watching crowd wryly quipped, 'Who the bloody hell is that woman standing next to Johnny Owen?' Straight to the point, down to earth, that's how they are in Merthyr Tydfil. In the quiet, panelled room, Johnny signed the visitor's book. For a Merthyr boy, this was a great honour and one he fully appreciated and savoured. As a token of their pride in his achievement and to mark the occasion, they gave the boxer a unique commemorative plaque. The quiet young man graciously thanked all concerned.

Johnny spent Christmas in 1977 reflecting on his achievements: he had won both the Welsh and British titles, and was number four in the top ten British boxers in the bantamweight division. He had also been named Welsh boxer of the year and came fourth in the 1977 BBC Wales sports personality of the year, finishing behind another true champion, David Broom, the magnificent international showjumper.

Johnny had been a professional fighter for just 14 months. His rise to the top had been unrelenting and remarkable. In the year ahead, he would dedicate himself to at least staying there. He could hope and dream for more, yes, but he would equally be satisfied with consolidating and improving.

A lot of talk about Johnny's next opponent began to surface. Since he had become a champion, things had changed a little. People had begun to look more respectfully towards any challenge to his title. They understood his class and ability, and were aware of the obvious threat he posed. His chances against other fighters would always be analysed in greater depth. Fights would be slower in coming. There would be more speculation than before. He would have to get used to that, take it in his stride. It was part of what was now happening to him, part of being professional. Johnny, though, paid scant attention to life's what ifs. He just wanted to fight. He approached the bouts with the philosophy 'When they're ready, they will let us know', then he could get down to training. It didn't really bother him who he fought. Bring them on and I'll beat them, that was Johnny's perspective.

The winter of 1977 was harsh and cold. Snow had begun to fall heavily after Christmas and Johnny's training was curtailed by the inclement weather. Luckily, he had bought an exercise bike and was able to get in the training he needed at home. He soon got fed up of all that indoors stuff though, and one morning, despite the snow being thick on the ground, he announced he was off out for a run. He put on a plastic suit with the trousers up to his armpits and headed off for his usual chase through the valleys. He returned a few hours later, having enjoyed himself. He had run miles and miles in the snow. The run involved a particularly steep incline called the Sanatorium Hill, an awkward local nightmare. He had managed to navigate that, too, and with ease.

Johnny's single-minded determination had once again come to the fore. He refused to let even the heavy snow interrupt his schedule. To him, it was an obstacle in his path. It got in his way. He'd removed it to ensure he could once again train as he wished. He knew where he was going. He had this quiet determination and sense of purpose about himself. He would not be dissuaded from his strict training regime, regardless of the weather.

The wider world would never really know how determined and stubborn the quiet and sometimes shy, introverted Johnny Owen could be. They could guess, but it wasn't the same thing.

Johnny needed to keep up his training schedule through all the bad winter weather because he was to meet Alan Oag from Edinburgh in his next fight. He met and beat him on 23 January 1978. It was an Eddie Thomas promotion and was held in Aberavon. The referee stopped the contest in the eighth round. It surprised a few that Oag had managed to last eight rounds that night. It was a comfortable win for the champion.

Johnny's next big contest was for Johnny Spensley Promotions and was held at the Marton Country Club, near Newcastle, on 27 February 1978. His opponent would be Antonio Medina, a Mexican living in

Spain. This man would be no bum of the month, no pushover for Johnny. He was a very good fighter and everyone predicted an excellent contest ahead. Dai Gardner was unsure about the fight, feeling at that particular time that the Mexican was too experienced for Johnny. After much discussion, though, he was persuaded otherwise.

Dai Gardner's instincts proved almost correct in the first round of the fight. Soon after the bell had sounded, the Owen camp quickly realised what they should have known previously: their opponent was a southpaw. The southpaw leads with the right hand and so can throw a left-leading boxer off his stride. Johnny was more than a little concerned at the end of the round. They hadn't done their homework correctly and therefore couldn't have told the champion. It was not good planning and should not, must not, happen again. Johnny asserted his class and authority on the inferior challenge of Medina. He regained his composure and went on to win the fight with relative ease, the Spanish-Mexican not having brought his best fight to the arena that night.

After that bout, Johnny took a week off and had a well-earned rest. He then went back to some light training in order to slowly bring himself back to peak fitness. Routine and discipline continued relentlessly, as they always do for the true professional boxer. Johnny didn't mind one jot and soon training began to take on a more serious edge. So did the sparring and roadwork. He ran literally a marathon a day through the hills and valleys surrounding his native Merthyr Tydfil. But the Sanatorium Hill was the most famous. Everyone knew how evil that hill was to run up. To walk or even drive up is hard work; Johnny Owen would run up *backwards*!

If he had decided to be a marathon runner instead of a boxer, then it is likely he would have made it to the top and become one of the best in the United Kingdom, if not further afield. But boxing was his life, his first love. It had got to him before any other sport, so there was never any real debate as to what Johnny would dedicate himself to. Some people have since said that he should have been a runner. If he had become an athlete or maybe a marathon runner instead of a boxer, then maybe things would have turned out a little differently. Well, there was never any question of that happening. Like all the great fighters, Johnny Owen was born for the ring. Just as Ali, Frazier and Hagler were.

The match fitness that Johnny Owen was achieving through sheer dedication and hard graft, combined with his knowledge of ring-craft and tactical experience, was the real long-term investment he made in his future as a boxer. Hard work is an investment. He had never swayed from that belief. He instinctively knew it to be true. But his dedication often overshadowed and clouded issues for some people. Many saw Johnny's potential in purely monetary terms. That's fine, it's a way of looking at things, but in order for that to work, you have to be good and fit to fight. Dedication to that end became Johnny's real investment in his sport. Nothing in this life comes easy; Johnny had worked that one out for himself. He would set out to prove his own theory had true merit.

Heddwyn Taylor had somehow managed to organise an unlikely title-fight challenge for the champion of Great Britain. For Taylor, it represented the promotional chance of a lifetime. It would be held at the Ebbw Vale Leisure Centre on 6 April 1978 and it would be the first time the Bantamweight Championship of Great Britain had been fought in Wales and the first time it had been fought between two Welshmen. For Heddwyn Taylor, this had been a grand coup, of sorts.

Johnny's opponent for the fight would be Wayne Evans – a strong fighter with a powerful punch, a good scrapper and a boxer with an excellent amateur record. It was a good match. He would stretch Johnny and test his claim to the title. The Owen camp drove the ten miles or so over to the Royal Oak in Ystrad Mynach for the official weigh-in. There was a problem. Johnny was 2 oz. overweight.

Wayne Evans laughed and teased Johnny vindictively over his weight problem, temptingly holding a glass of orange juice to his mouth, using cynical pretence, urging his opponent to drink. Johnny didn't like Wayne's attitude one bit. Even so, it didn't interfere with his concentration. All is fair in pre-fight hype, after all. So, he let Wayne Evans have his day. He went to Dai Gardner's house nearby and, with a little training, lost the few ounces he needed to. If Johnny had been angry at Evans's public jibe, he wouldn't ever have shown it and he certainly wouldn't take that anger into the ring with him – that would be fatal. Losing one's temper in a boxing ring is a crazy waste of energy. It gets a boxer nowhere. Even so, he would not forget. Through boxing skills, tactics and talent, Johnny would attempt to make Wayne Evans come to understand his mistake in jibing him. He prophesied a win, and win he did, but the fight was not as smooth going as the champion expected. Wayne Evans proved to be a slippery and difficult customer for the champion to shake off.

The first three or four rounds were about even as the boxers settled. Johnny had maybe stolen the second, but by the fourth Johnny's left hand was beginning to tell as it remorselessly beat at Evans's head and body. In the fifth, Wayne caught Johnny with a good punch on the ear and, when the champion returned to the corner, his ear was bleeding. He immediately began to have trouble with his hearing and there was some concern at the end of the fifth. The ear was patched up quickly though, and Johnny went back in for the sixth round, determined to put things right. He did just that in a superb display of temperament, skill and unbelievable stamina. Wayne Evans was no match for the champion in the end and by the tenth round, Johnny had stopped the challenger. He had won. It had been a really tough fight. A struggle at times. But the defence of his title had been successful and that was all he had come to do. Even the beaten Evans applauded his opponent as Johnny walked around the ring in a lap of honour, as a token of respect for his fans. The very next morning, he went to see his doctor to discuss his ear problem. It seems the blow had punctured his eardrum. The problem soon cleared and Johnny never had any trouble with it again.

Johnny's main nickname was the Matchstick Man. This was because he was so thin and skinny. Some would say he looked like a skeleton. Johnny's fans accepted that that was how their champion was. This was his make-up. This is what he looked like. They knew how tough he could be and what a great boxer he was, so it didn't matter a bit to them. Those who saw him strip, ready to box, for the first time, however, were often shocked by his outward appearance. Dick Owens was often criticised for the way Johnny looked. As though he could do much about that! Some said he was too thin. For others, he was too fragile. And so it went on. They were not to know how strong and fit and powerful the young man really was. How could they?

Even Johnny's manager, Dai Gardner, was harassed because of his charge's slight appearance. There were those, fight fans or otherwise, who wanted Johnny's career stopped before something happened to him. Again, that section of the community believed Johnny was too thin and too frail to box. They could not understand how someone of Johnny Owen's light physique could possibly be in the fight game or indeed even allowed to compete. Sometimes the phone wouldn't stop ringing at Dai Gardner's home. Especially in the run-up to a fight or in the period after a fight when publicity photographs were in all the newspapers or on the television. Still, life went on and Dai got used to it; the more Johnny excelled in the boxing ring, the less intrusion everyone suffered. There wasn't anything that anyone could do, other than carry on regardless, and take the criticism and the praise in the same level-headed manner. It's the best we all can do with life.

Dai Gardner had organised the next fight for Johnny against Londoner Dave Smith at the National Sporting Club on 12 June 1978. Smith was a very experienced, rugged fighter, extraordinarily brave, with the heart of a lion, and known to all as an excellent competitor. Johnny was up for it. It would be an exciting encounter scheduled over 15 rounds and was just the kind of bout the champion needed at this time. It would be tough and competitive, aggressive and close enough to keep him on his toes. After a few weeks of hard training, Johnny set off for London and was as well prepared for Smith as he could be. On the night, Johnny put his preparations to good use in the ring and, with his usual skill and tenacity, won the contest quite easily on points: 79–75. Apart from a brief moment in the fourth round when Smith hit Johnny with a barrage of body blows, there was no way the challenger was going to win. Magic Johnny was just too good for him. There could be only one point of concern in the Owen camp that night. Johnny had had chances to finish Smith off, but he didn't. The press covering the fight asked questions about the champion's punching power. He was now the complete tactician, but he needed to display a punching ability. This was a minor criticism, though, and nothing to concern anyone deeply, but it would have resonated in the Owen camp nonetheless. However, the fight against Smith was a better win than it looked. The champion was improving all the time. The Johnny Owen story continued to flow.

There was now a lot of talk flying around Wales concerning the possibilities of a European and a Commonwealth title challenge for Johnny. As usual with these things, the gossip was way off the mark. One minute it was on, the next minute it was off. Rumour countered rumour. First, Eddie Thomas was to promote it. Then it was Heddwyn Taylor. No one quite knew what was going on. Johnny kept up light training 'in case it happened'. He ticked over with a daily routine and waited to see how everything would develop. In the end, it was Dai Gardner who came up with the only genuine offer.

The Commonwealth champion was an Australian called Paul Ferreri. He had said yes to the proposition of Johnny Owen fighting him for the title – as long as they fought in Australia! Johnny turned the opportunity down. The consensus was that Australian judges were prone to 'home' verdicts and tended to be lenient towards their own boxers. Hardly surprising, since most countries also bore that criticism. Whether it was the truth or not, no one could really venture a guess, but it was a long way to go to get beaten. And if the rumours were to be believed, that's what would happen to them – they'd get beaten. And what then? Johnny figured it wasn't worth the risk.

Instead, Dai Gardner matched Johnny Owen at the Café Royal on 25 September 1978 against Wally Angliss from Harrow. Johnny stopped Wally in the third round of the fight. It was a relatively easy victory, but a victory that seemed to rekindle rumours of an impending Commonwealth title contest. Johnny went back to Merthyr Tydfil after the fight for a couple of weeks of well-earned and much-needed rest. Then, out of the blue, thanks to promoter Heddwyn Taylor, the

Commonwealth title fight was back on. It would take place on 2 November 1978 at the Ebbw Vale Leisure Centre. Ferreri had decided to fight in the United Kingdom. He was confident and many impartial observers reckoned he was right to be.

Ferreri received a good press upon his arrival on Welsh soil. The hacks were praising him to the rafters. The majority agreed that he'd be too experienced for Johnny, too crafty for him. They also promoted the fact that no British boxer had ever beaten him as a way to undermine the Welshman's chances. They cited Ferreri's record, his shot at the world title and his 70 contests. Whereas Johnny had a mere 16 professional fights. On paper, the Australian looked the man to watch. Some journalists, though, were sticking with the local boy, reflecting on the potential of Johnny, his dedication and skill. It remained to be seen who would turn out the better fighter in this perfectly balanced contest.

Johnny's first encounter with Ferreri was in a TV studio. They had been invited on to annoy each other, egg each other on and, of course, to sell tickets. There, for all to see in front of the world, Ferreri gave Johnny an inexpensive little boomerang. After a little wisecracking at the expense of the boomerang, Johnny then asked Ferreri something. 'You've got a little girl, haven't you?' Ferreri nodded yes and Johnny pulled out a Welsh doll. 'Give this to her.' Ferreri thanked his opponent, but decided nonetheless to have the last word and a bit of fun at the challenger's expense. He turned to Heddwyn Taylor and asked where would *he* be sitting during the bout. 'Ringside,' replied the promoter.

'Tell me which seat and I'll put Johnny in your lap. Free of charge.' Now that's confidence. It brought a wide smile to Johnny Owen's face.

The fight took place on 2 November 1978, as announced. Holding such a prestigious contest in this part of the world gave a much-needed boost to the Ebbw Vale economy and its boxing fraternity, and the local boy was deemed favourite, at least in Wales. When the fight began, the hall was full. This was a much-anticipated bout. Rated the boxing match of the year, it was to fulfil its billing tenfold. No one could have predicted or expected such a wonderful contest. It was sublime in its presentation of the finer arts of the sport. It was as good a display of bantamweight boxing as had ever been seen on Welsh soil, indeed anywhere. The referee was left with virtually nothing to do but watch. As *The Sun*'s chief boxing reporter, Colin Hart, stated at the time, 'The sixth round was boxing at its very best. The BBC film of the fight should be shown to amateur coaches everywhere to help teach promising youngsters.'

Johnny Owen went all the way to the 15th round before taking the title: 148–145. The remarkable young man from Merthyr Tydfil had become Commonwealth champion in only his 17th professional fight. It was a great night. He had outpointed Ferreri memorably. Johnny was carried from the centre of the ring to the dressing-room shoulder high. His name was flashed around the world. He was in the top ten world-class bantamweight boxers at that moment. The crowd gave him a standing ovation. It was one of the finest nights Johnny Owen would ever have.

As 1978 came to a close. Johnny could well have sat back in self-satisfied calm. He was becoming quite a celebrity now and not just in Wales. All through the boxing world (America aside perhaps), the name Johnny Owen had begun to resonate with fighters and promoters alike. But despite being the champion of Great Britain and the Commonwealth, despite his obvious celebrity, Johnny Owen changed little as a man – he still helped around the house, was always respectful and charming, and continued to train and work at his craft as hard as ever. He was fast becoming an example to up-and-coming young boxers. And the accolades were also coming in thick and fast.

Johnny was runner-up in the 'best boxer of the year' contest, as voted by the London Ex-Boxers Association. Allan Minter beat him to the title – one of the few contests Johnny did lose that year. Even so, he was presented with a silver tray as a consolation. Also, the Ferreri versus Owen match for the Commonwealth title was voted second in the 'best boxing contest of the year' category. High praise, indeed. There were favourable reports in all the newspapers and most carried positive articles about the young man as the year tumbled to its inescapable close. What for next year? they all asked. Well, there was always the European title. That would seem to be next on the checklist.

Johnny Owen would have agreed with all that speculation. The European title was very much in his sights and, as usual, accompanied by the on–off speculation that always seemed to walk hand in hand with the big boxing events. The bar-room promoters and boxing enthusiasts all wanted Johnny to go for champion of Europe. But that would have to wait a while. The speculation would have to remain just that – at least until 1979 had officially opened its doors of opportunity. For now, the Owen camp relaxed into the Christmas period and ignored the rumours and counter-rumours.

Johnny received a wonderful 23rd birthday present on 7 January 1979: he was voted the 'best young fighter' of 1978 by the prestigious Boxing Writers' Club. He was only the third Welshman to receive it. The other two were Howard Winstone and Dai Dower. He received the award at the Club's 28th annual dinner at Quaglino's in London on 24 January 1979. After Johnny had been presented with the award from the Club's chairman, Walter Bartleman, he made a speech. A first, if ever there was one! If the audience members were surprised at the quiet man of boxing saying anything more than thank you, his father and manager were astonished.

'Boxing is said to be a one-man sport,' Johnny began. 'Don't you believe it! You need a team behind you, and I'm very lucky to have Dai Gardner as manager and my father, Dick, as my trainer.' Then, to bring them all back to the reality of boxing training, Johnny finished off with, 'I sometimes think that they are slave-drivers, but it's all for the good.' It was a touching moment for all those who had been on board from the outset. It allowed a time for thought and quiet reflection to creep in and briefly disturb the daily routine.

The news they had all been waiting for came out of the blue, almost. The contest for the European title was definitely on. It would be fought on 3 March 1979. The location was to be in the home country of the champion, Juan Francisco Rodriguez. It would take place in Almeria, Spain. No one was happy with the venue. Their unease would have paled into insignificance had they known what was to unfold during their time there. For now, though, they were happy it was on. Happy to be fighting for the European bantamweight title.

The happiness and elation would be short-lived. It would turn out to be one of the most trying times for Johnny Owen and it would be an experience that would test each and every one of them to the limit.

11

MEXICAN TUESDAY

Hot, red, blistering sun burns through wispy-grey early daytime mist. New fresh-morning vapour monotonously rises from the ground, a haze of blurred, condensed steam. An occasional birdsong hangs pathetically in the air, in the silence of the unused and not-yet-confident morning. This bird will not sing for long. She will be drowned out, silenced, relegated to the almost alive. Her song will be flattened, her ascendance shattered, her hopes for the day dissolved in disappointment, when the monster awakes.

At the very centre of the great city lies the Plaza de la Constitucion (Zocalo), the hub of the city's downtown area. It is Mexico City's historical centre. Presiding resplendently over all events in the famous square is a stunningly beautiful architectural masterpiece of 'Old Spain', the Catedral Metropolitana (the first stone was laid by the Archbishop Pedro de Moya y Contreras in 1572). The cathedral stands on the northern side of the Zocalo, facing the city. As you look at it, at its left is a small precinct of shops, restaurants and cafés. Opposite the eateries are the great buildings of the government, the parliament, and the offices of diplomacy and foreign affairs. Close by is Calle de la Moneda, the 'Street of the Treasury'.

Directly outside the cathedral gates, in line with the surrounding iron fencing, on the pavements and some on the roads, cheap-souvenir salesmen ply their wares out of makeshift, put-me-up stalls. They are a noisy, colourful, crowd-pleasing addition to life on the square. A police presence regularly marches back and forth, holding a line, ensuring peace, preventing tourists from harassment and guarding a right of way for all. In contrast to all the meaning, hidden or otherwise, that the iconic Roman Catholic cathedral advertises, desperately hungry beggars, the old and infirm, Mexican Indians and mothers with young children sometimes literally at their breast, or screaming to be changed of soiled clothes, sit around pleading and waiting for handouts. The cathedral, with its varied and colourful people, was astonishing to behold. I would return and take in the experience in much greater depth on more than one occasion later that week when all the work was done and there was peace to do so.

Dylan and I were drinking coffee in a café facing the intriguing (to us they were, anyway) government buildings when we first heard the chanting and vitriolic, slogan-driven protest sounds. Dylan was waiting to direct, waiting for action, taking five. The sounds seemed familiar in their passion, agitated in their rhetoric, angry in their intent. I wondered where Arthur Scargill, that great leader of the working classes, was right now. The shouting seemed to be emanating from the rear of the cathedral and getting ever closer to our position on the almost-empty square. Gradually, the advancing threat became louder and more hostile. It appeared a major political demonstration was heading our way. Primarily, all seemed quite surreal, unreal, something to laugh off, so we joked about the onset of revolution, about being Graham Greene-like heroes stuck in some British Empire outpost. We laughed at the idea that we should change into white suits and Panama hats, and light up a cheroot, drink gin and 'it' whilst waiting for the peasants to arrive and storm the palace, cool as you like. The angry voices got louder and louder. The additional volume meant a change of tone. We began to seriously wonder.

Dick Owens had left to be shot at the other end of the square. Not literally shot, that is. Not with a blindfold and famous last words.

Things hadn't got that bad. We were, after all, only into our second day here in Mexico City. Give us time. He was being shot for the film: Dick strolling across the square, walking amongst the people, by the cathedral looking in at God, that sort of thing. It was hot and quite humid, sweaty weather for pink, well-wintered European Welsh folk, and extremely tiring to work in. I sipped my coffee. Dylan and I could just make out the trio of Ynyr, Huw and Dick Owens. Huw had been busy lining up Dick for the camera. He had sorted out the shot he wanted after waiting till both he and Dick had agreed it was all right. The action, discussed with Dylan earlier, could then be set in motion. When that was done, cameraman and producer headed towards us at the café. Dylan had taken up his position at the edge of the square to the front of the table, close to his drink. As soon as he saw all was ready, he began guiding both Huw and Ynyr as to where he wanted the sequence of choreographed events to unfold. Dick stood stock-still and waited. The idea was that Dick Owens would quietly, pensively and with great dignity make his way across the Plaza de la Constitucion. The camera would do the rest. The fuss about the shot was to do solely with the background.

The voices got louder. I noticed an armed police or army officer on the roof of one of the state buildings, the sun reflecting menacingly off his mean, black-as-coal, no-entry sunglasses. I mentioned the discovery of the guardsman and the gun to my fellow travellers. I felt that, what with the angry demonstration heading our way and the Mexican government arming itself nearby, it might be a good idea if we positioned ourselves elsewhere for now and should maybe think about postponing the shot (before we were shot) for the day. After the briefest of configurations and an even shorter discussion on the pros and cons of that suggestion, it was agreed to continue. This was just a little 'political spat', nothing to worry about; a mere 'peaceful demonstration', a wholesome display of democracy, probably a tourist thing. The three well-used and well-known reasons for not stopping any form of filming were also trotted out. Number one, this is show business and the show must go on; number two, the budget; and number three, there's a schedule! So, on we went. Dylan shouted

'Action!' and Dick walked across the square towards Huw and the camera. Then all hell broke loose.

The voices at last arrived in the square. Hundreds, no thousands, of working-class Mexicans, totally cheesed-off at creeping privatisation, the loss of their jobs and the removal of welfare benefits, descended upon the Zocalo. Dick Owens, totally aware of the situation, but unfazed, kept walking towards us as instructed. Huw kept filming. Dylan had slowly begun to see the funny side of it all through the edit lens. From my position, outside of the bubble that was being created by the documentary team, the funny side had quickly become the hilarious side.

The angry mob entered the square in great haste. As a crowd, they moved much more swiftly and efficiently than you would have imagined a sizeable group of untrained individuals could move. They entered directly behind Dick Owens and it looked for all the world as though Dick was leading the revolution. 'Che' Owens had come all the way from Merthyr Tydfil to Mexico City to take control of the workers and bring down the government. What a shot! The man on the roof, the man in the tar-black, no-entry shades, raised his rifle butt slightly and was stealthily joined by a second armed officer. A third came through an opened French window, shuffling in lethargically behind his two comrades, lighting a cigarette at the same time. Company and reinforcements had arrived on the roof for the once-lone guardsman. I pointed out in my own panic-driven paranoid way that we might have a problem or two to contend with. 'Look up there!' I urged.

We debated the situation but it didn't take long before the penny dropped. 'It might be a good idea if we moved on. Perhaps cameras, indeed recording equipment of any kind, might not be the best of instruments to have around right now. Governments are a bit touchy on recording the treatment of protestors during uprisings of any kind and we were foreigners after all, we shouldn't forget that. It might be in all our interests if we pushed off to another place. Don't you think?'

Producer, director and cameraman looked first at the crowd – hostile, fermenting, morally superior, menacing, ugly, loud and intent on bother – then they looked at the equipment – valuable in its own right with irreplaceable film. The logic of the situation became ever more apparent with each glance at each part of the equation. Worried heads shook and common sense soon prevailed.

The rest of that Tuesday in Mexico City was spent going from one set piece to another. Dick Owens, the principal character, was put through his paces and kept busy almost without a minute to spare. He was filmed inside taxis, walking up dirty, grubby lanes, looking at fresh fruit in marketplaces and sitting outside restaurants sipping coffee or tea or beer. He was filmed walking under archways, examining architecture, outside the hotel, inside the hotel and trying to cross the jam-packed road. He had been caught on camera for almost the whole of the day. For him, the day must have been tiring and unfriendly and boring. But necessary. It was all part of why he and we were here, after all. At the end of the day, we all retired for a well-earned dinner. At the conclusion of the meal, Dick had to be interviewed once more. When the talking and questions were over, the day's work was done. Each of us could relax if we wanted to.

The following day, Wednesday, was the big day. The highlight of the week's filming. The film team had gone downtown to Lupe Pintor's house and to his gymnasium to tie up any loose ends that remained. While Dick Owens and I sat enjoying a drink, they were working on yet another reconnaissance mission, making sure everything was set fair for the meeting between Dick and Lupe Pintor less than 24 hours hence. One had to admire their industry and creative input. I asked Dick how he was feeling about the week ahead, now that he had had a taste of the film world. I asked him if he was looking forward to meeting the ex-champion of the world. He didn't register too great an enthusiasm for the world of film, but of course he was looking forward immensely to meeting Pintor.

With all hints of jet lag disappearing fast and the first real day of filming behind us, it was easier to sit and reflect. Easier to chew the fat and take in the surroundings, try to understand the place that is Mexico City. You see a lot in a day, wandering around in a foreign town without any hard and fast plan to adhere to. And what you don't see, you feel. It washes over you, a place like this. Mexico City had grown from a population of five million in the '60s to an astonishing twenty million today. What had happened? What changes in society had taken place to encourage such an incredible invasion? They poured in from the countryside at the rate of 1,000 a day, all of them migrants hoping for a better life. Surely, they'd enjoy the green grass of the country much more than this? What must it have been like to box here, to be a fighter here, in those early days of the city's incredible growth? I put the question to myself, rhetorically. I had no answers, just ideas.

Little wonder, we mused, that Mexican boxers were so strong, so powerful, so intent on winning. They had to be. Fighting a way out of Merthyr Tydfil was one thing, but to fight your way up the ladder here? Well, that had to be a very different experience. Lupe Pintor was a Mexican Indian. Indigenous peoples the world over had been the butt of economic exploitation whenever and wherever the New World entered their domains. The scandalous takeover of land and culture by European settlers still haunts much of America to this day. The New World had been born largely through the efforts and gullibility of those indigenous cultures. The New World Spain had arrived and conquered an Old World Mexico. The Mexican Indians had no chance. The Spanish, still hugely influential culturally, have long since ceased to rule directly. Now, it was the United States that interfered and messed with everything. California was still a sore point in Mexico.

Dick and I both agreed that there were enough similarities with Wales to allow us to begin to understand why Mexico had bred such wonderful boxers. There were similarities of culture, imperialism, industrialism and, strangely enough, religion. Wales had its fire-and-brimstone chapels; Mexico got its orders from Rome. Poverty and mass unemployment were also part of the equation. The fighting spirit of Merthyr Tydfil was in this city too and we'd seen it at work with our own eyes just a few hours previously in the square during the demonstration. Boxers come from a certain sociological place; a certain corner of modern society breeds and nurtures them. Being Welsh, one could see why Mexico City would breed champions.

Dick assessed that Johnny Owen would have done well here. As a fighter, he was a true master of his craft. Johnny also loved the game; the game of boxing was his life. He understood the dangers involved in fighting for a living, as all boxers do, or at least should do. It's very much like sitting on an aeroplane, awaiting take-off. The stewards stand there performing their safety drill for us, showing and telling us what to do if an emergency were to occur. We are told that what we are to embark on is indeed a dangerous event. How many of us actually take a damn bit of notice of those safety warnings? And why do we not really care? Because we love to travel. Discovery is in us and is as much a guiding force for us as any other in our lives. No journey is without risk and we take the chance because life is dangerous and risky, and deep down we know that if it wasn't we would not be living it properly. The force that drove Johnny Owen was similar. He took the journey because he loved what he did and he had to. Not to do so would have led to a miserable life, an unforgiving life. Boxing is dangerous and there are risks involved that all boxers should be made aware of. The same applies to life.

The fight game, though, still often puzzles. It still causes even the best of us, with good intentions and its future at heart, to think deeply about its reasons for existing. How do you get to love a sport that is very often violent and life threatening? How does that work? Dick and I talked on. And much of what was said between us eventually began to make sense. We worked out that you probably grew to love the game because it is so difficult, so skilful, so honourable and so very exciting. There are many, many reasons for a boxer to want to box. There's so much more to it than the violence and danger.

Yes, you must try and hit your opponent and not get hit yourself. And yes, you can get hit and hurt and cut, and sometimes it can be downright hazardous there in that boxing ring, in extreme cases fatal. What you must not do is place these dangers at the front of your mind. You should always be aware of them, but they mustn't rule your actions. Instinct is very often a better instrument of safekeeping –

instinct, good training and preparation are very often all a boxer will need. Fear and nerves should be there, but only to help, not to hinder. For it is they and anticipation that inject the adrenalin.

In this sport of boxing, you go into the ring boxer against boxer. Once there you try to inflict harm on your opponent, knock him out if you can and generally endanger his very right to exist. On the surface, it is crazy behaviour. But after the contest, you love one another like long-lost brothers and you forget all the pain you inflicted on each other. That brings to the fore one of the major reasons why the meeting with Lupe Pintor was so important for Dick Owens.

The meeting was not just about wresting and resolving something from the past, or knowing that Pintor wanted this to happen because he needed help to come to terms with his own life. Nor was it important because it enhanced the memory or reputation of Johnny Owen in any way, shape or form. It was none of those things specifically. It was all of them, and more. Dick was there as his son's representative, there as a spokesman for the gladiator who couldn't make this meeting himself, there to say hello and rest assured the champion gladiator of Mexico City. Respect between brothers in arms transcends the ages, eclipses life and death, never fades or dies. And for Lupe Pintor, there is much respect.

That respect is born out of an inner knowledge, natural to fighters of all kinds, that those outside the ring, those not truly involved, can never gain access to. This knowledge is unique to each fighter and it is learned and nurtured. No one can teach it. Boxers alone know how fast things are in that ring, how a punch can hurt, how difficult it is to skilfully avoid your opponent round after round, and how much stamina is needed for the task in hand. They alone know of the courage they must draw on for such a fight and courage is very often so difficult to summon. They are no different from any of us in that department. This knowledge brings them emotionally close to their opponent after the bout has ended. It is a gladiatorial respect that runs through the sport (and is not only evident in boxing).

We ended our Tuesday discussion on that true note of respect and decided to step out for a short walk in the Mexican traffic. It sped by, as it does, day in, day out. We walked around the block, got off the main road and took in the better air of the quieter lanes that meandered gently on the rolling hills behind the hotel with their clean, brightly painted houses and their small grey satellite dishes. We needed the walk. It was to be a tough day at the office tomorrow. Time to think and reflect is always useful time and what better way to do that than to walk. That day had been one of humour, hard work and good heart.

Slowly, we headed back to the hotel. Still talking, but not too deeply or too seriously about anything much, still learning in the land of the Aztec, and still very aware of the presence of Johnny Owen over all we were attempting to achieve. One can learn a lot about the world on a Tuesday in Mexico City.

12

THE REIGN IN SPAIN –
STAYS THERE!

Compared to the rest of Europe, Almeria in 1979 was like the Dark Ages. Women all dressed in black going off to the mountain to gather water, pails on their heads; men sitting lazily on the town square talking and spitting; beggars begging; ancient old fruit markets and bullrings and loads of evidence of El Presidente, General Franco. That was everywhere. They'd have had him back in a minute. At midday came the siesta and everyone disappeared. It was a sad, old place.

With all Johnny's training finished, he boarded a flight from Heathrow Airport bound for Spain. With him, and tending to all the arrangements and immediate travel needs, his trainer and manager. It was 1 March, St David's Day. It seemed like a good omen. All of them wore leeks on their lapels, as is the tradition with the Welsh on that day. It's either green and white leeks or golden daffodils, one or the other. They figured the leeks might give the proceedings a little edge of nationalism, which wouldn't harm the fight publicity when they arrived at Spain's glorious capital city, Madrid. From there, the Johnny Owen Championship boxing entourage would take a shuttle flight on to their destination.

Almeria is situated in the south-east of the Spanish peninsula, bordering Granada and Murcia. As a claim to popular fame, Sergio Leone and Clint Eastwood's classic Western *A Fistful of Dollars* was shot there in the 1960s. The filmmakers felt it a strange-looking place: cold (but not weatherwise) and empty, wild and eerie. Inland, Almeria has an almost lunar landscape of desert, sandstone and dried-up riverbeds. At the time, it was a perfect location for the new kind of Western that Eastwood and Leone had planned. It was a place of vivid contrasts, a place of pure conflict. It gave the impression of being a place where life was cheap and of death turning up everywhere. It is important to emphasise that this, of course, was just an impression and not the reality, but it is the kind of impression that struggles and hardship bring to a place, and Almeria was a place of struggle back then. At the end of the day, the filmmakers chose Almeria because they felt it had the right feel about it for that first Spaghetti Western. They chose right.

As things turned out, Johnny Owen and his training and management team would soon agree with more or less everything that attracted Sergio Leone and his star cast to Almeria for their 1960s adventure. Except that, for the boxer, there would be very few positives to take back home with him from his experiences. As well as quickly discovering the strange geographical landscape and hostile idiosyncrasies of the region's native peoples, the Owen camp would also find that grabbing the fistful of dollars due them at the end of their exploits would turn out to be as difficult as the fight itself. Indeed, it would be as troublesome for them to nail the money as it was for the characters in the Eastwood film to secure their loot. They were a far cry from the opulence and 'fair play' of the Café Royal, or the clinical modernity and home support of the Ebbw Vale Leisure Centre. This was new and foreign territory for all of them, about as far removed from Merthyr Tydfil as one could get.

Almeria's capital city, home to some 125,000 or so souls, is also called Almeria. Today, it is a highly organised, bustling, modern European city. It is a place of culture and learning, a place of high tourism and technology. In 1979, it was a vastly different place. Spain was in post-Franco mode and approaching its first free elections for 40 years. Almeria was behind the times. Spain itself had developed along very different lines from most other Western economies during Franco's years of leadership. Indeed, Spain contrasted greatly with its more liberal political ally the United Kingdom, and Almeria in particular had developed slower than most other regions of Spain.

On paper, this looked to be hostile territory for any visitor from beyond the country's borders. There would certainly be little or no support for any boxer trying to get his hands on a Championship title in this part of Spain. The reception Johnny Owen would likely get when he entered the bullring (and it was a real bullring) would be hot and very likely touching upon the dangerous. There would be little welcome, not too much goodwill, from the Almerian people – that much was known for sure. All the considerable research and investigation they had detailed and gone into beforehand indicated that this would be a rough and hostile journey. Dai Gardner and most of those impartial observers along for the ride, some to write, some to film, felt that there could be problems ahead on this trip.

One or two surprises greeted them upon arrival, good and bad: the hotel was excellent – first class, five star; the food on offer was awful – third rate, no stars. It was not up to the standard required for a serious athlete in training for a major event, that was for sure. The Owen camp had come prepared, though. Again, the team's research into the trip, conditions and venue had paid off. They had worked out beforehand that the food might not be 'up to it' and so had decided to prepare Johnny's nourishment themselves. Dick Owens had brought a supply of good old British fare, just to be on the safe side. It proved to be an excellent decision.

The Spanish promoter in charge of the fight caught up with them very soon after their arrival in Almeria. He offered to take the whole of the Johnny Owen team out to dinner on their first night in Spain. The promoter needed to inform them all of what they might expect over the next few days. It was the best way of approaching problems, clearing up any minor difficulties that might be causing concerns, and answering questions the promoter's guests might need to put to him about the fight and their surroundings. It was also a way of dealing with any messy business relating to status and money during their stay before potential problems surfaced.

Dai Gardner was advised that his boxer could use the gym facilities provided. It would be the same gym that the champion Rodriguez would be using. Johnny would be allowed to use the facilities each day after noon, but they must, at all costs, first wait for Rodriguez to finish his training session before commencing their day's work. Dai Gardner agreed in principle. The next day, Johnny Owen arrived at the training venue at midday, the allocated time, and he waited, and waited, and waited. For a full hour, he (and everyone else) stood in the steaming-hot noonday sun. For that first hour, nothing happened. They were kept outside, and far away from the gym and the training facilities. The Rodriguez camp had won a tiny, but significant, battle of the mind. The Owen contingent began to wonder. This was not how it should be.

On the boxing front, another old problem reared its ugly head again – weight. Johnny was a fraction over the 118-lb limit for the bantamweight division. Dai Gardner ordered him to run up and down the hotel back stairway to try to shift the ounces. However, Dick considered, for whatever reason, that Johnny was the correct weight. He and Dai began to discuss the rights and wrongs of the situation, especially when Dai had – in Dick Owens' mind, unfairly – instructed Johnny not to have any breakfast that morning. While they were arguing and discussing the merits of the manager's decision, Johnny Owen was getting on with the innovative exercise plan, removing the weight anyway. Pressure? Not a bit of it! Johnny Owen rarely felt any kind of pressure.

Weight problems were not restricted to the Owen team, though. The opposition was finding things a little difficult, too. The problem of weight was about to disrupt the preparation for this Championship bout and explosively so, for it was not only Johnny Owen who had weight problems. Serious concerns began to surface at the weigh-in.

Rodriguez, arrogant and unreceptive to any sporting advance on behalf of the challenger, stepped onto the scale. He was overweight. A bucket and a half over, as some wag pointed out, and he didn't seem to care. A frantic argument over the champion and his obvious weight problem began between the authorities, the Rodriguez camp and other impartial observers from the media. Rodriguez didn't seem to give a damn. A shambolic, frenzied tit-for-tat debate ensued between those who were advocating fair play and a reasoned contest, and the Rodriguez camp, who more or less told them to take it or leave it. A casual Rodriguez walked straight through the mêlée to the bar. There, he demanded a litre of orange juice. Dick couldn't believe it. The Spaniard couldn't care less. Dick took Johnny's arm and led him away. In his opinion, it was a madhouse.

Dick, the impartial and UK observers, and the travelling media who were there to cover the fight, assumed the European Championship bout would not go ahead. The champion was overweight and flaunting it and surely the match could not be taken seriously any more. Rodriguez's real weight problems couldn't be cleared up overnight. Dick and Johnny went back to their hotel room and began preparing to leave. They waited until Dai arrived with news. When he eventually came, the news was not what they both expected. The fight was still on. Dick was stunned. He questioned how it could be still on, since Rodriguez was overweight. Dai explained that the officials in charge of the promotion had now stated that Rodriguez was all right to box. There was nothing further he could do about it. They could stay and fight, or go home with nothing.

So, it looked like the litre of orange juice had not put any further weight on Johnny Owen's already overweight opponent. It was pretty obvious to anyone who knew anything about boxing and the build-up to any fight that the pre-match rules and regulations were being flouted. It seemed a very mysterious way to go about preparing for any fight, let alone a fight of this magnitude. Johnny was fine. He would get on with being as well prepared as he possibly could be. Dick Owens was shocked, as was Johnny's manager and the press entourage. Dick and his son had much to think about before agreeing anything further. After a period of isolated decision-making, they decided to go ahead with the contest. The fight was on.

The venue for the European Bantamweight Championship was to be a functioning bullring, a place of death. It was a perfect venue for a fight in Almeria. It was as though the venue was reflecting its location. Whether deliberately or otherwise, the promoters had spelt the challenger's name incorrectly on the posters so it read 'JHONY OWEN'. It seemed they were purposely having fun at the expense of the foreigners from Wales. Each time they approached something new, something they had to attend to or something to do with the fight, they would be confronted with some anomaly or another. It was becoming clear that the problems for the men from Merthyr Tydfil would go on and on all the way to the fight itself.

The Owen camp arrived at the venue and made their way into the building. As they walked to the dressing-room, the crowd, in a nasty, deliberately ungenerous mood, booed and shouted abuse at Johnny (at least they didn't throw anything). If Johnny Owen hadn't understood it before, then he should now. Everyone should now understand the predicament. The odds were stacked against the challenger both physically and psychologically. They'd be very lucky to get any kind of result this time. They had better brace themselves for a rough time and a probable defeat regardless of the boxing. A knockout seemed to be the only way they could get home with the spoils. It was the only realistic tactical advice that could be given to Johnny in the dressing-room before the fight. But then he'd worked that out for himself by then.

On top of everything else, the dressing-room they had been given to use for the fight was actually the matador's chapel, a small prayer room painted stark white. There was not much else in the room apart from an altar, a bench and a table. They were not sure if they had been blessed by being put next to God or were being prepared for a culling in the coming fight. No one knew what to say or what to expect.

By then, the innocent crowd that had come to support Johnny Owen from Wales were becoming not so innocent. They sensed that the fight was not just about the contest in the ring. They began to realise that there was another, in many ways more serious, battle going on beyond the fight they had come to see. At first, in their naivety, they assumed that Johnny would be fine in Spain; that everyone played by the rules of boxing especially at Championship level, where the bouts were regulated and watched so carefully. In Almeria the rules of boxing seemed to be heading out of the window and it wasn't over yet. Those watching carefully could envisage that there were still a few mind games and problems to be played out by the Rodriguez camp before the match was over.

Soon, though, it was time for the fight itself: Rodriguez versus Owen. Rodriguez had boxed only 13 times as a professional, fewer than Johnny Owen, but he was a hugely experienced fighter. The Spanish authorities had kept Rodriguez as an amateur, much as the Soviets and the Cubans used to do with their boxers. They needed him to win medals for the country at the Olympics and in Europe, and he had duly obliged. It was a sign of a changing Spain that Rodriguez could box as a professional. It was a sign of Rodriguez's skill as a boxer that he had risen to be champion of all Europe in such a short space of time and in so few bouts. Rodriguez was known throughout Europe as a boxer of supreme skill. Johnny Owen would have had his work cut out to beat this Spaniard on a level playing field. What chance could he possibly have here in the rigged-bout atmosphere of pre-fight Spain? This European Championship challenge would be the Welshman's biggest test to date, both as a boxer and as a man.

And so, after an inexpensive bill of amateurs, entertainers and relatives, Johnny Owen entered the ring, where he was welcomed by a mixture of jeers and slow, intimidating handclaps. He was unconcerned. He had a job to do. The fight was to be fought over 15 rounds.

The first round turned out to be no more than a warm-up, the two boxers giving and taking as much as they got. When Johnny came back to the corner at the end of the round, however, Dick smelled the unmistakable whiff of wintergreen massage oil. In boxing, that is not a smell to be welcomed. At least, not during a fight! The wintergreen had come from Rodriguez's gloves. Johnny had been affected. His eyes were smarting, stinging. Dick complained loudly to the referee about the oil. The referee ignored him. The crowd became annoyed at what they regarded as Dick's unfounded, incessant complaining and soon turned their venomous attention towards the trainer.

To try and calm things down, and set to rights the indignities being imposed upon the Welsh fighter and his trainer, the veteran BBBC representative inspector Harry Vines came to the Owen corner to find out what was going on and to see if there was anything he could do to help. On his way there, he was jeered, shoved, pushed and abused. The police were in the corner next trying to throw out Vines. The whole event was rapidly turning into a surreal nightmare, a farce. Dai Gardner tried to explain to the anxious police officers who Harry Vines actually was and what it was he represented. The police relented slightly, but they still insisted Vines go back to his seat and stay there, in the name of security. Vines was dumbstruck, but did what he was told. The fight was descending into madness.

In the rounds that followed, Rodriguez was holding and butting almost continuously, he even screwed a thumb in Johnny's eye. The referee, interestingly, did not issue one single warning to the champion. It was by then becoming obvious that, no matter what they tried to do that evening in Almeria, things were to go against them. Only a knockout could win it for Johnny and that was not even 100 per cent certain to be successful. Not the way things had gone and were going.

Next, enter Rodriguez's brother. He waltzed over to Johnny's corner, bravado to the fore, as bold as you like, to tease, taunt and generally wind up the Owen camp even more. The brother got in everyone's way, and yelled and screamed at Johnny as he made his way back to the corner at the end of each round. This interesting character was the mild one of the family, though. Rodriguez's other brothers were standing behind the judges as they marked their cards. Two for us, one for them, or else, seemed to be the implication. At this stage, it looked like Johnny would have to shoot Rodriguez to win. And even then . . . who knew?

At the start of the tenth round, Johnny Owen was sent out to box as normal, but Rodriguez wasn't at the centre of ring to meet him when he got there. He hadn't come out of his corner to fight. Deciding to have a rest or a cigarette maybe? Johnny stood in the middle of the ring for a full minute and then, in a performance filled with satire and antagonism, he started bowing to the crowd and blowing kisses. He was mocking his opponent and the audience supported this sham. He remained alone, there in the centre of the ring, for what seemed like an age. The crowd were clapping and laughing, enjoying the Welsh team's discomfort. This was a travesty of a contest. When it finally got under way once again, the boxers fought to the distance, to the end of the 15th round.

This kind of thing cannot happen today, here in the twenty-first century, where satellite television and communication technology ensures we see all things as they happen. Nothing escapes the eye of the camera these days. Rodriguez would never have got away with it today. Back then, it was just possible to steal a little from your opponent, if the scam had been organised properly beforehand. This fight, although looking a shambles, had actually been well organised by those who wanted to win it at all costs. There was no doubting their commitment to that cause.

When it was over, as the scores were being totted up, most pundits gave Rodriguez no more than four rounds. The general consensus around the bullring auditorium was that Johnny Owen had come to Spain and beaten the European champion fair and square. He was in a different class that night and it had showed throughout the fight. The judges gave Rodriguez the verdict. It was expected and disgraceful. There was no use in complaining, at least not yet. There would be time enough for settling old scores with this champion.

Johnny smiled bravely in public after the defeat, but behind the scenes there was only deep despair. He had won and proven himself a class above his Spanish opponent, but he had still come away the loser. Between the three men – Johnny, Dick and Dai – a decision was reached.

No matter how long it took them, no matter what they had to do to get there, who they had to fight – they vowed that they would eventually claim the European bantamweight title, which they believed was rightfully theirs, from the man that had snatched it from them so blatantly. When they had set this wrong right, all that would remain before them would be the Bantamweight Championship of the World.

13

AND NOW – THE WORLD!

I was very pleased that night. Johnny looked world class. I always knew he was. I was the proudest man in Wales after that fight. Except for his dad of course.

Dai Gardner, reflecting on the European title return fight against Juan Francisco Rodriguez

What do you do when you're down and out, fed up, browbeaten and disappointed with life and the unfairness of it all? When, all around you, long-held dreams look distant, lost and forlorn? What do you do when you're not sure of what to do next, when you have been dumped and knocked off course, and have to rethink and replan and reinvigorate those dreams of old, and are not in the mood for any of it? What you do not do is go for self-pity, bitterness and resentment with your lot. Down that road lies ruin, and a bleak and uncertain future. Everything that happens does so for a reason. Good or bad, the die is cast. The trick in life is to accept things, and to move on and continue to do what you believe is best regardless. Pick yourself up, dust yourself off and start all over again. That was the mantra and the way things had to be after the Spanish non-event of Almeria. Johnny Owen had not been beaten in Spain. He had lost nothing. He had been robbed.

The media and impartial observers agreed that the Spanish adventure had been a fiasco. The Welsh Area Boxing Council discussed every aspect and detail of the fight. They took evidence from Johnny's camp and sifted through copies of all the Spanish and European newspapers that covered the bout that night. Harry Vines, the BBBC's man at the fight, gave a lengthy account of what had happened in the ring and of the staggering incidents that occurred outside it. Vines described the decision as the worst he'd ever experienced. For all this reaction and universal angered support on behalf of the defeated challenger, there was nothing much anyone could do. They could condemn and deplore all they wanted. Juan Francisco Rodriguez was still champion. But things change fast, in life as in boxing, and Johnny's time to deal with Rodriguez would come around soon enough. They would be patient, wait and steadily build for a return match. Johnny Owen would get his second chance at the European title and that second chance would be all he would need.

It was different now. Everyone knew something for certain, like never before. Out of the shambles of Almeria came the absolute knowledge that Johnny Owen was the best bantamweight in Europe.

Soon after the dust had settled on the Almerian catastrophe, Dai Gardner placed a new option on the table for his fighter to consider. He'd arranged a contest with a top American boxer, Jose Gonzalez. The fight was to be held at the National Sporting Club on 19 April 1979. It was good news that was not to last. Johnny trained hard, got himself ready and up for the fight, but it was called off soon after Dai's optimistic announcement was made. Gonzalez had weight problems. They were, so Johnny's boxing manager was reliably informed, non-reversible and too severe to allow Gonzalez to continue. The bout was immediately cancelled. The American had decided to fight lightweight. That was the end of that. Except that Johnny Owen was now match-fit and left with no one to box. Another opponent had to be found for him, quickly.

A young boxer from Finchley, London, called Lee Graham was quickly guided into place. The fight was rearranged for the same date in April 1979. Johnny Owen was as fit for this match as he had been for any other, even though young Graham was not considered the greatest of opponents. At least, not by those reporting the fight. Johnny Owen took the fight as seriously as any other and afforded the young Finchley fighter the respect he deserved as a professional boxer earning his living in the ring. For all Johnny's care and consideration, it was not a real and genuine contest on the night. Lee Graham was no match for the strong, experienced champion. The contest was fought well and in good sporting spirit. Johnny Owen won comfortably, on points: 79–77. Graham had fought hard and well, and had got much closer to the champion than most believed he could. Still, Johnny had been in charge throughout.

Johnny Owen's next opponent was quickly readied. It would be the French boxer Guy Caudron. The fight would take place on 10 May 1979 at the Pontypool Leisure Centre in the heart of the industrial south of Wales, just a short train journey along the valley from Johnny's home in Merthyr Tydfil. Caudron was a tough, experienced pro, one of the best in Europe. It would be a good contest. Johnny would be tested. He had little time to return to ring fitness after the Lee Graham fight, but as usual Johnny threw himself into training and ensured he was back to as near to peak fitness as possible in time to face the Frenchman. The press, spectators and critics said Caudron would definitely test the Merthyr boxer. They were right. Caudron's examination was a thorough one. He fought well and displayed knowledge of his craft, and an experience that Johnny had to find ways of dealing with. He made Johnny Owen work consistently hard throughout the fight in order for him to gain any ground at all. Although it was a tough battle in there, and although Caudron fought hard and fast, Johnny never really looked like losing. From a spectator's point of view, it might not have appeared such a great fight. In the end, Caudron held him for the distance. Johnny came away with a 99 points to 97 victory. It wasn't easy, but it was hard fought and deserved.

In his private life, away from the ring, Johnny Owen had continued to hold down his steady job. Now that he was becoming busier with his ring commitments, however, the factory job had become almost surplus to requirements and the young professional boxer couldn't commit himself to the factory as he used to. His boxing life had begun to take over and had become a priority. Johnny had kept the job because he felt he owed something to the company that had supported him so well over the years. He didn't want to let them down, but the manager of the factory had become concerned by his employee's regular absences and began to air those concerns. Johnny could see the company's point of view, resigned amicably and devoted himself 100 per cent to boxing from that day on.

At last the news that they had all been secretly waiting for came. Johnny Owen would soon be defending his British and Commonwealth crown for the third time. He would now get the chance to win outright the coveted Lonsdale belt. His opponent would again be Dave Smith. No one gave him much chance of success. No one really expected him to beat Johnny. Heddwyn Taylor, Johnny's old promoter friend, had arranged the fight for 13 June 1979. It was to be held at the Double Diamond Club, Caerphilly. Johnny quickly went back into training in earnest. To win the Lonsdale belt outright had been a long-held dream for the Merthyr boxer. If Johnny should win, the belt would become his property. This fight was something special for him. The Lonsdale belt is given outright only to boxers who successfully defend their titles three times. It's a sign of a great champion to have successfully attained the distinction of outright winner of a belt.

On the day of the contest, Johnny and his father went through the usual pre-match rituals. They had a light boxing round, they weighed-in at the Royal Oak in Ystrad Mynach. The previous night, Johnny had become very serious about the fight. This was a big one for Johnny. Winning the belt outright had been one of his main ambitions at the outset and one of the things that had driven him on and on through the years of hard slog in training. He could now achieve that ambition. All he had to do was just beat Smith and the belt was his. The idea that he was so near to a goal he had set for himself so many years ago was playing on his mind a little. For the first time ever before a fight, the young man was showing signs of nerves. He was a little hyped up.

'One contest at a time and all are equally important.' That's the mantra and the recipe for success in all sports. Dick and Dai would have been very aware of that. So, it is likely that his trainer and manager would have delivered that advice loud and clear to the young man the night before the fight, and told him to be cool about it all, to calm down and to breathe deeply. They could well have added, 'Forget ambition but use it.' The simple things had to be reiterated and remembered: take one fight at a time, concentrate on getting through, try not to place any extra importance on the task – that could be fatal – do not take anything for granted, always treat your opponent with due respect. All these things he needed to be told. Johnny would have understood perfectly well that, as long as he turned up ready and able to fight, there was no reason on earth for him to lose the bout. Nerves would have settled quickly.

After a good night's sleep, refreshed and easier in his mind, fit to bursting and physically at his peak, Johnny Owen headed for the Double Diamond Club for the fight itself. Dick was probably more nervous than his son on the way to the venue. Yet he must have felt, deep down, like so many of the Welsh fans of the great boxer did at the time, that the Lonsdale belt would soon be Johnny's. He ought to win it.

This was a special title fight for Wales and the pull of the local boy meant the hall at the club was full to capacity that night. It was a good start. At least the promoter had done well! Soon, the fight was up and running.

Johnny went after Smith almost from the echo of the first bell. If anyone ever doubted the young man's appetite for the fray, or questioned his determination to win the Lonsdale belt, they were, by the evidence of their own eyes, soon silenced. Johnny gave all he could to the fight, and more. In a remarkable display, he saw to it from very early on that only Johnny Owen could possibly win. Poor Dave Smith took an awful lot of punishment that night. He was (thank goodness) eventually retired by his trainer and manager in the 12th round. Smith's head was swollen by about two inches from its normal size. The referee had no option but to stop the bout for fear of the challenger's health and future. Johnny Owen had been much too strong for the Londoner. He had won his Lonsdale belt. He was exultant.

After this impressive performance, Johnny continued training, but in a different way. It was summer, and he gave his time and energy to charity and good causes. He took part in various 'fun' runs and attended fundraising initiatives all over South Wales for a variety of organisations. He kept himself busy, but soon the summer sun faded and it was time to get back into the ring again. The momentum towards a return with Rodriguez was now paramount to the plans Dai Gardner had for his champion fighter. The European Championship was at the heart of a much bigger dream, but they had to overcome Rodriguez first.

Johnny's next opponent was Neil McLaughlin. McLaughlin, his old Londonderry adversary, had developed into a good, strong fighter, known for his skilful boxing. He had improved no end since the last time the two boxers met in 1976. It would be a proper match, fought in good boxing conditions. The fight was held on 17 September 1979 at the Albany Hotel, Glasgow. Despite McLaughlin's immense bravery, Johnny won the contest by 100 points to 95. McLaughlin was never to defeat his old adversary. They parted as friends, each with a great respect for the other's skills.

After the lull of the summer, Johnny was booked to fight almost immediately. He was matched against an American boxer, Isaac Vega, rated at number 13 in the USA. The fight was supposed to have taken place on 4 October 1979. Amazingly, when the Owen camp arrived at the Ebbw Vale Leisure Centre, the fight venue, ready to fight Vega, they discovered their opponent had been changed. Isaac Vega had pulled out and not a word had been said to them about it beforehand. They were given little by way of excuses and even less time to make up their minds about the alternative to Vega. The promoters had parachuted in another challenger. If they were to fight at all, they would have to fight someone completely different and, of course, unknown to them. The boxer waiting to face the champ was a Mexican, Jose Martinez Garcia. Both Dick Owens and Dai Gardner tried to find out what they could about the new opponent, but both were unsuccessful. Neither of them was able to throw up much in the way of good, solid information on the challenger from Central America. Although they were not best pleased (an understatement), they decided to proceed with the bout, feeling Johnny needed a fight and the experience would be worth its weight at a later date. The champ quickly got on with the job in hand. The referee stopped the contest in the fifth round. It turned out to be an easy win.

Johnny's next fight was against New Yorker Dave 'Baby' Vasquez. The fight took place before a full house at Ebbw Vale Leisure Centre on 29 November. It was a hard-fought battle between the two men for the most part, the Welshman finally easing out a good winner on points. A year earlier, Vasquez had fought world champion Lupe Pintor in San Antonio, Texas. Pintor had disposed of the challenge in two rounds.

Johnny had to wait till 1980 for his next significant contest. His opponent was Glyn Davies from Llanelli, a tough South Wales mining and steel town, not dissimilar to Merthyr Tydfil. Davies was a tough old pro (old for boxing, that is) who'd been around a bit and seen a lot of champions. The fight took place on 22 January 1980 at the National Sporting Club in London. The referee stopped the contest in the fifth round in Johnny's favour. It was another easy victory. 'I have been beaten by the next world champion,' was all Davies had to say at the end of it.

At this point, Johnny decided to invest some of his hard-earned money. He bought a small grocery store on an old Merthyr Tydfil council housing estate called Galon Uchaf. Dick Owens, wearing his father's hat, was not wholly in favour, but wished the young man luck nonetheless. Johnny was pleased with his investment and turned out to be an excellent stock buyer. The shop did well. Things were really looking very promising indeed for the young man. The fights were going well, the shop was making money and, as a bonus, to put the icing on the cake, Heddwyn Taylor had come up with a very special offer for Johnny Owen: a return match against Juan Francisco Rodriguez, the Almerian European champion.

The Owen camp snapped up the offer. At last, revenge against the Spaniard was on the cards. The fight for the Bantamweight Championship of Europe was to take place on 28 February 1980. Rodriguez, realising his pay days were virtually over for him in his native Spain and that, in all probability, no one would fight him over there anyway, gave the choice of fight venue to the promoter and the challenger. The bout would take place at the Ebbw Vale Leisure Centre. Johnny Owen was ecstatic at the news. It was just what the doctor ordered.

The leisure centre in Ebbw Vale was packed on the night of the contest. Not a single highly prized seat was left available. It promised to be a memorable night. For Wales, this was one of the fights of the century and the local press insisted that this was so, hyping and pumping up the fight news day after day, elevating its promise higher and higher to fight fans and beyond. Every possibility had been covered, every possible outcome predicted. The press had done well for the promoter and the two boxers. Nothing would be left to chance in the fight preparations. History would not be allowed to repeat itself in any way, shape or form. Juan Francisco Rodriguez and his team of trainers, managers and handlers would have no chance of perpetrating the same deceptive conditions on Johnny Owen that had been played on him in Spain the previous year. This fight was organised, the money properly addressed and there were no dirty tricks. The crowd would not be antagonistic (at least, not to Johnny Owen), and Rodriguez would get a full and proper idea of what a fair fight should be like.

Johnny Owen fought like a true hero that night. He outboxed the European champion in every department. The fight, slow to start, soon fiercely got going, much to the delight of the enthralled audience. The fighters spent the first round bobbing and weaving, weighing each other up, working each other out. By the second, Johnny had Rodriguez already worried as he pursued him relentlessly ever forward. The challenger wanted to get after him; Rodriguez held on, wincing under the pressure. The champion caught Johnny with a couple of right-hooks to the face in the third, but the Matchstick Man rallied with a series of successful jabs as a counter-attack. The fourth and fifth could be called even. Rodriguez seemed more confident than he had been earlier and duly fought that way. At the end of the sixth round, Johnny surged in with rights and lefts to the body as Rodriguez struggled on the ropes. But the champion survived the onslaught yet again. Throughout the next three rounds, Rodriguez showed the Welshman his experience and Johnny missed a lot – the rounds were even. It was to be Rodriguez's swan song because for the remainder of the fight it was all Johnny Owen. One-way traffic. The challenger showed his incredible skill and stamina to a defiant Rodriguez in a finale worthy of a champion. Rodriguez must have known throughout the closing stages of the fight that it would be his last as the champion of Europe. Typically, Johnny had kept his best till last.

Rodriguez got what he deserved. A three-pronged verdict from the judges voted unanimously against him. Johnny Owen had won on points to become the new bantamweight champion of Europe. Tearful, he was lifted high above the crowd. In defeat, the ex-champion Rodriguez was hugely complimentary to the Merthyr Tydfil boxer and strangely, after all that had happened between them in Almeria, magnanimous in the way he took the loss of his crown. After the fight, reporters asked Johnny if it had been the best of all his performances to date. 'I hope not. I want better than those!' was his response. When asked if he was off to celebrate, Johnny replied, 'I'll have an orange juice. That lot [pointing at those around him in the dressing-room] will celebrate for me!' Johnny had exacted sweet revenge on the European ex-champion. He was the European champ now.

After the fight, the Owen camp had a well-deserved party to christen the title win. They were all agreed that there was never any doubt about the result of the fight with Rodriguez, never a worry at any time during the bout, never a problem with the great man's capacity for boxing and its craft. To a man, they insisted that this wonderful Welsh boxing machine would soon become the champion of the world. Surely, it was now only a matter of when, not if, and a matter of timing and good fortune as to the date he would meet the current champion. 'What a day that will be!' they all agreed.

Soon after the successful Rodriguez challenge, and after a short period of relaxation, Johnny's next battle in the ring was announced. He was being kept busy. It was how he liked it to be. The next fight was to take place in London against John Feeney, a very powerful, talented boxer and an old adversary from Johnny's amateur days. The Commonwealth and British titles would be at stake. Feeney lived in London but was originally from Hartlepool in the north of England. He had been unbeaten in 17 fights and would be a stern test for the champion. He was younger than Johnny at 22 years of age, but had never boxed over 8 rounds. Stamina would play a big part in Johnny's preparations for this defence of his titles.

In his favour, Feeney had a quick left-hand and was talked up as a great puncher. Johnny did not believe Feeney to be as classy as Paul Ferreri or as cagey as Juan Francisco Rodriguez. Dick and Dai held the same view. No one considered the possibility of defeat, but no one took victory for granted either. On the night of the fight, the champ showed absolute conviction and determination to the cause. Both titles were on the line, after all. This was a serious fight. Feeney could do nothing more than stave off the relentless pressure and hope for another day. In the end, Johnny Owen went on to win a well-fought contest on points.

Almost as soon as the bout against John Feeney had ended, news came to them of a new fight offer. It was the news that they had all secretly hoped for, but believed might never come their way. It had been a patient wait. Londoner Micky Duff, one of the top promoters in the fight game, indeed one of the best promoters the fight game has ever seen, approached the Owen camp with a sensational offer of a world title fight in the United States. Micky Duff had been associated with some of the best fighters of the past half-century or so: Muhammad Ali, Sonny Liston, Mike Tyson and Sugar Ray Robinson to name but a few. He had also guided 19 boxers to World Championship success. The offer could be taken seriously and was soon accepted. Johnny Owen was now only one step away from being world bantamweight champion.

The real dream, the dream of dreams, was now on. Johnny would prepare as he had never prepared before. All the years of hard work and learning were almost at an end. The rainbow beckoned and the young boxer from Merthyr Tydfil in the South Wales valleys stood ready to take his chance. Every morning from then on was a joy to the boxer. He could prove his worth on the highest stage of all. Johnny Owen was happier than he had ever been. His time had come.

But cracks, though not serious, were beginning to show within the decision-making team of manager and trainer. Preparations for the fight would be stressful and fraught with tension, and nervous energy would play a major role in the participants' mood swings. This was the real big deal after all and a real big test for all of them. They had nothing to compare this venture with. They were, all three of them, in new territory yet again. Dai Gardner had decided not to take sparring partners to Los Angeles. Dick did not agree. Dick had wanted Johnny's usual sparring partners to accompany them to America. Dai wanted the Owen camp out in Los Angeles two months before the fight on 19 September. They would use sparring partners provided for them over there. Dick disagreed again. He saw no point in that exercise. It flew against everything they had done previously. He believed that there was no need for them to be in LA two months ahead of the fight. Dick also objected to accommodation arrangements. They were to stay at the Gala Motor Hotel, which was located in downtown Los Angeles. Dick felt the location to be wrong and dangerous. He was overruled. After many debates and arguments and furious discussions about this, that and the other, a compromise was reached and some sort of peace broke out. Dick earned some concessions and Dai gave in on some things.

One of these concessions was that they would not leave two months before the fight to train and settle in Los Angeles. They would fly out the week before the fight and ensure all training schedules were fulfilled at home. Johnny would be ready and super-fit before they left the United Kingdom. Many were critical of the decision to fly out so close to the fight date, citing dehydration, jet lag and acclimatisation problems as reasons for their concern.

In fairness, the arguments they went through during the initial preparations for the fight are not uncommon. There are very often behind-the-scenes disagreements in sport. The way they prepared for the fight had no bearing on the way things eventually went for them in Los Angeles. Both Dick Owens and Dai Gardner wanted the best for their boxer. They would have done anything to make life easier and better for Johnny. They were both dedicated professionals. It is easy in hindsight to criticise some of the decisions made at that time. When you know the result, that kind of criticism is easy. They prepared for the fight as best they could so that Johnny Owen would be fit and ready on the night.

In the run-up to flight-time, they would change their training and eating times to correspond with Pacific American time. The night before the flight out, Johnny's grocery store had been broken into. The family kept it from him. They'd tell him on his return. At 5.30 a.m. on the morning of their flight to Los Angeles to fight for the Bantamweight Championship of the World, five cars pulled up outside the home of Johnny Owen. The cars were filled with supporters. They had arrived to wish Johnny and the team the very best of luck with their sporting adventure. The fans played 'We'll Keep a Welcome in the Hillside' full blast on their car stereos and woke everyone up for miles around. The supporters had also decorated the streets around Johnny's home town with flags and bunting in his honour. This was a supreme send-off for the champ. He was their champion, after all, and here they were showing him what they genuinely thought of him. More cars full of supporters followed Johnny and his small but faithful entourage all the way along the 200-mile journey to Heathrow Airport in London.

The flight left at 11.30 a.m. Johnny didn't eat anything until they were over Iceland. By then, they were flying on American breakfast time. Soon, they would be in Los Angeles.

14

GLADIATORS (2)

The Avenida de los Insurgentes is the longest continuous city street in the world. It bisects Mexico City more or less from north to south. It is the city's most important artery. To the north, Insurgentes leaves the centre past the train station and close by the northbound bus station, to sweep out of the city via the Basilica of Guadalupe and Indios Verdes. It is impossible to walk this city street, end to end, on a hot day in summer. Only a madman would try. It would be crazy to run. No one would run. Not even if the sun was down. Not even in the early morning. Not even if their life depended upon it. No one except, perhaps, a world champion professional boxer, in training for the defence of his realm.

It is the crack of dawn. An almost empty horizon stares at us across the brow of a hill in a quiet, slightly run-down, neat and tidy, almost litter-free city suburb. Everything around us is drab and near predictable – to an experienced inner-city dweller that is – and magnificently big. It is also intense and slumbering, fragile and dangerous. The city sits quietly brooding as it patiently waits for the fun to begin. Like a bomb expecting to go off, it ticks away the seconds, knowing the outcome of the day ahead better than any of its hopelessly lost, system-tied clock-watching inhabitants ever will. It needs no permission to exist. It lives even without the living. It has no explanation and it cannot be explained.

Easy footsteps approach the barren line at speed, running. They are both hurried and relaxed, and carry with them the obvious air of experience and the sound of deep, controlled, laboured breathing. Through the misty haze and onto the centre of the brow of the hill, as though choreographed for effect, comes the lone figure of a running man. His attire is pure sports. Dressed in a heavy, hooded tracksuit with pristine white training shoes, he looks like an athlete should look. His features are powerful and intense. His face etched with pained and strained perseverance. He tests his lungs, tests his capacity to run, tests every muscle in his legs and body to drive him on. He breathes well and feels good. He feels like a champion. He feels like he is on top of the world.

He has learned that running is no more, no less, than an act of balance. He has learned that you have to get to the point where legs and lungs work together in harmonious unison, in an equal state of exertion. He has learned not to stop and stare or pause to pose or sign his name. He has learned to take notice of nothing that will affect the way he spends this time. He commands himself to override everything he can in order to implement the one major lesson he has really learned on his way to the top of his professional greasy pole: the condition of the body is everything.

He glides slyly, almost automatically, past all those up-and-early risers who choose to stand and stare at him in awed recognition. He runs straight through them. As though they were not there. Some call after him, 'Hey, champ!'

He allows a smile to break through the concentration in a comfortable, reflective silence. Champ is a word he likes very much. Champ is a word he feels he has earned.

He is short and stocky with slightly gelled jet-black hair. Moustachioed and clearly Mexican, he seems uncomfortable but not overly so in the blistering heat of the late summer's morning. Autumn beckons, but still the high summer sun refuses to relent. Each day brings the same bad news. It will be hot and dry in the morning, hot and humid by mid-afternoon, hot and steamy by night. It seemed to him like it had always been this way. That it would never end. It felt so hot you wished some days to be free of it. Free of the insanity of the heat and of life lived under its power. He continues on. He hits the concrete road hard like a hammer, with sore feet and with a force that makes his shinbones shiver. This man is a professional boxer. This man is a champion of the whole wide world.

He loves to run. Running is where he feels most free. It ennobles and emancipates, heals and educates. When you run, you think. When you think, you ask. When you question, you learn. He asks all the time, every day, each day. There are questions of self-worth and direction, questions of dependence and independence, questions of life, of love and God, and questions that need hope in their response to encourage survival. All and more he asks daily, wilfully, unfailingly. The half-developed, not always illuminating, sometimes confusing and very often puzzling answers returned to him, via his own thoughts, make the running even more worthwhile. There is no light on some days. On others, the future looks like heaven. The loneliness of the runner has always been compatible with the development of the inner voice.

Sometimes, he thinks that there is more to life than this. He feels he wants more than just the title of a world boxing champion. He is not being disrespectful in these thoughts. Not showing ingratitude or being blasé in any way about the sport that he loves so much and which has given him everything. He is just exploring this world of his to its limits.

It began as a fight out of poverty. It began as a battle against a society that cared little if he were alive or dead. It moved on to his being recognised, as his potential as a fighter came good and met the right eyes. Quickly, that recognition turned to respect when he became a champion. It had been a tough and sometimes heartbreaking fight from nowhere. He had made it. Left all the crap behind. And he had made money too, a fortune, and all the trappings of social wealth fell into place with it. They call him 'the Champ' now. The respect is overwhelming some days. But still he wants more. That's why he fights on. That's why he keeps going. It's not just for the cash. It never was. Nor is it because he likes to train hard and run and keep in shape. Nor is it for the respect offered to him, by all his people. Yes, they're his people now. He must go on because he wants more, much more. But he doesn't know what that 'more' is yet. That panics him sometimes. He feels that one day it will come. A light will shine into his eyes. Then he will know what to do. Then he will know.

He thought that by now he had defined and attained his goals, but deep down there was something missing, always something missing, and an emptiness that did not explain itself. Fame was not as he thought it would be. He'd found that fortune did not always buy what a man wanted. So he fought on and kept himself in shape and prepared for the big day. The big day, when he would discover what he felt he lacked. It would reveal itself. He was sure. If life was tragic, then Mexico City was a tragedy he had escaped from. If all men's lives end in failure, then maybe his will not. Maybe he will be different. For him, maybe things would turn out differently. Maybe this gift of world champion meant something else. Maybe he should use his fame in another way. Maybe he should use his fame to create some kind of good in the world. It felt like he had been given this thing, by forces that he could not see, that were checking his every move, but not telling him what he should be doing. As though playing with him to see if he would respond as he should. It felt like that some days.

He represented something when he fought. He knew that much. Especially when he fought away from his home. He represented his people – the Indian, the true Mexican. He felt this new fight coming up in Los Angeles would not really test him. He felt that. Not as a man! It wouldn't test him as a man. It should be easy and should present him with little in the way of professional difficulty. He would be fighting before his people in Little Mexico, in the Olympic Auditorium, their stadium. His opponent would have to be made of iron or steel to win. He would have to be courageous and lined with stamina, and have a determination to beat him that bordered on the insane. He would have to be unique to trouble him.

Around a bend in the road, he goes. Effortlessly turning a corner, on the planned and well-worn route. He glides into a thin, cobbled inner-city street. The road ahead of him now is long and narrow, and dips steeply before rising at the other end. It's like a giant inner-city U-bend stretching out before him, challenging him, begging him – 'Take me! Take me now!'

He ploughs on through the rising, agonising heat. It's been a freakishly hot summer and the arrival of September has brought no respite. A car passes close to him. It sounds its horn. The supporters within call out to him – 'Respect, Champ! Respect!' Respect is the biggest word here in the slums and suburbs of the old town. The town he sprang from all those years ago. To fight here is to defy fear and pain. It had been tough and he'd largely done it alone. But he had done it. That was the point. He holds up a golden hand to the gleeful supporters in thankful response. The car disappears quickly from view. He gives it no more thought.

He passes the same small Catholic church he passes each day. It springs up to his left out of the rubble and half-dead dogs, and it always surprises him. Always catches him off guard. Halfway to the end of the run, halfway home, it sits there reminding him, today and every day. He crosses himself devoutly, says a quick and sudden Hail Mary. He does not stop. The condition of the body is everything.

He runs and runs and runs. It's a metaphor for life, he thinks. All of us just run and run and run, and stupidly collect things only to leave them all behind. The only thing he collects is boxing titles. And the one he must now defend is the one that's most important to him. He is in training. He is preparing his body for a new challenge. He is in serious mode.

Perspiration pours down his face and falls to the ground below. It almost instantly disappears in a small cloud of evaporated steam, into thin air. There is no thinner air than that of Mexico City, not in the whole wide world. So he has been told. He is soaked through, his training tracksuit drenched, but this is how it should be. He could not, would not, accept anything less.

In dedication and hard work lies the sureness of victory. It's what he believes. What he instinctively knows to be true. He lives by it. If you do not put in the work, how can you win anything? How can you be anyone? He understood this long ago. From the very beginning, he knew the secret. He had talent, yes. He had dedication too. He had the love of the sport as well and he aligned the three with hard work. It had been the secret of his awesome success. He saw many of his compatriots fall by the wayside because they did not work, did not take life seriously. They wanted respect from others when they did not respect themselves. How can that be? There is nothing the world will give you for free. You have to work for it. There are no free lunches.

In boxing, it's tougher. Tougher, yet more straightforward. You know where you are in boxing. If you do not work, you are beaten. If you are beaten, you are nobody. To be nobody in Mexico City is to be less than nothing and so he works and trains hard and runs and runs and runs. And it makes him feel good. It makes him feel on top of the world, like a champ.

'Hi Champ!' shouts the snotty kid at his elbow. He wonders where the kid came from, out of the blue, like that.

'Can I run with you?' The Champ says yes. Soon, there is another kid, then another, then another, then another. They form a line behind the champion of the world, their hero, and every single one of them has a huge and deeply ecstatic smile pasted on his face. The smile widens their light-brown, hungry, lean features and turns them into angels. His heart warms to them and now he is smiling too.

On the corner of a close, near a run-down, dilapidated street sits the boxing gymnasium. Next to it a 'Bar' sign flashes 'Budweiser'. It's a hard place to live. You can see that. A stranger should not venture there alone, nor get lost in that neighbourhood with a back pocket full of dollars. This is not a place for tourists. The street is uninviting, even more so in the heat. Rocking chairs sit stilled on the porches of the tired old buildings. A half-starved dog crosses the road with no fear of traffic, yet.

The boxer slips into view around an old building at the end of the street. Behind him, five young boys in training too are on the run of their dreams, with the champion of the world. Without pausing, he jogs onto the wooden pavement, runs past the old, starving dog, heads for the boxing gymnasium and, again without a pause, slides straight through the opened side door that leads into the temple of fitness itself.

His hard work continues behind closed doors now. That it continues and will be arduous goes without saying. What happens next is not for the squeamish.

One by one, the young kids that so adore him follow him into this new world. One by one, the five new gladiators of Mexico City make their way, hearts and minds, into the boxing ring at the centre of the universe.

15

KING LUPE

Lupe in full flight is tenacious, ruthless and vicious. He will chase you and he will catch you. There is no escape from his supreme greatness in the ring. He will hit you in the heart, in the kidneys, in the abdomen and, if you let him, he will hit you on the chin. Lupe will slip, parry, catch you inside, spin you and clip you hard on the side of the head. He will box your ears and not rest until it's over, and he is the superior fighter. Hopefully, you will know when he comes for you. If you don't know, your legs will. Hopefully, you will still be wide awake when he arrives. If you are not asleep, you soon will be.

Lupe Pintor was born in 1953, approximately. No one really knows. It's a Mexican mystery. One day he arrived. What else is there to know? At least, that's what he says. He comes from Cuajimalpa, Mexico. Cuajimalpa, or more formally Cuajimalpa de Morelos, is one of the 16 *delegaciónes* (boroughs) into which Mexico City's Federal District is divided. It is located on the western edge of the district, bordering the State of Mexico. He has always lived there. He always will. It is his home.

Lupe Pintor has a nickname. He is called *El Indio de Cuajimalpa* – 'the Indian from Cuajimalpa'. He is of the indigenous Mexican people. The name has always been there, too. As far as back as he can remember, it has been with him. It has travelled alongside him forever and still remains to this day, and it can be used to enlighten any self-respecting Mexican who doesn't quite understand who it is you wish to talk about. Mention El Indio de Cuajimalpa and your prospective tourist guide or friend will know in an instant who it is you mean.

In Mexico, in Pintor's neighbourhood, where the powerful humiliate the weak and to survive means to physically defend yourself in everyday life, every day of your life, young men with high spirits are driven into boxing. Hundreds of them fill the downtown boxing gyms all over the city. And there are many boxing gyms in Mexico City. More 'fighters' queue outside in the alleyways waiting for their turn. Each boxer waits for his chance. Each waits to prove he is better than any of his comrades ever will be. Each has one thing in mind. To one day become world champion.

Lupe Pintor began his boxing life in a gym in Mexico City. An ordinary backstreet boxing gym. Each day, he would queue with hundreds of others to show what he could do. Mexico City is an even more fertile breeding ground for fighters and boxers than Johnny Owen's Merthyr Tydfil. In Mexico City, the competition is severe indeed. All Lupe Pintor needed to get going in a place such as this was an opportunity. An opportunity to make his mark. When that day of opportunity arrived, he grasped it with open arms. Two powerful, closed fists, lightning reflexes and stunning upper and lower body movements did the rest. He was never an amateur. He was a professional fighter, with a capital 'P', almost from the word go.

He started his official professional boxing career in 1974 when he beat a highly rated compatriot, Manuel Vasquez, by a knockout in two rounds. It was a sensational beginning. It was the beginning, the old pros noted at the time, of a champion in the making. Maybe even of a world champion in the making. At the time, Vasquez was a very well thought of, young up-and-coming fighting prospect. Lupe was given little or no chance that night, but he came through with flying colours.

He was fighting in ten-round matches as soon as he could. As soon as they would let him. Much as Johnny Owen was. And very like his counterpart, Owen, Lupe Pintor was a boxer in a hurry. Not for him the safe route of bum of the month. There would be no conservative safety-first thoughts, no small pay cheques, no easy ways to the top for Lupe Pintor. He believed, as all great champions believe, that he was born for greatness. He would gamble and take on anyone because, deep down, he knew that he could beat anyone. He was, from his very first moment in the ring, a champion awaiting a crown. He waded into the world of professional boxing as though he'd always been there. As though he belonged there. Yes, this was the place for Lupe. This was where he belonged. He had found his dream. Now all he had to do was fight for it.

His very first ten-round match came as early in his career as his second bout when he beat Francisco Nunez (a contender) by a decision, on points. By his fifth fight, he had suffered his first loss, beaten on a disqualification against Magallo Lozada, a hugely experienced fighter and a talked-of title challenger. He got over the defeat quickly and learned much from it. He won his next eight bouts, seven by knockout, including wins over Juan Diaz, Rocky Mijares and Willie Jensen. These men were no mugs. They were all marked and rated fighters. Pintor was gaining valuable experience from internationally respected boxers at a very early stage in his career. Again, much as the contender, Johnny Owen, was doing in Europe.

Lupe Pintor first boxed the future world bantamweight champion, Alberto Davila, on 25 February 1976. He lost that day to Davila by a decision in ten rounds. A result that brought him no disgrace at all. It was a proud and courageous performance. He then won 21 fights in a row. Among the fighters he beat during that run of success were Nacho Beltran, Evaristo Perez, Eduardo Limon (who is the brother of two-time junior lightweight world champion Rafael 'Bazooka' Limon), a man who later beat Juan LaPorte, and Antonio Becerra, a Mexican regional bantamweight champion who had beaten Salvador Sanchez.

He travelled to Puerto Rico next and lost a ten-round decision to the Dominican Leo Cruz, a future world junior bantamweight champion himself. Back in Mexico for a comeback fight, Pintor lost for the second time in a row, this time to Wilfredo Gomez's rival Jose Luis Soto, by a decision in ten rounds. He would ensure that this run of two defeats would not be repeated in a hurry. Indeed, if he had anything to do with it, which of course he would, it would never be repeated. His recovery was swift and he embarked on another winning streak: five knockout fights in a row. You wouldn't have wanted to mess with Lupe Pintor at that time. He was on his way.

After beating Livio Nolasco in six rounds, he became the WBC's number one bantamweight challenger. He had come a long way in a short time. Even in terms of Mexican boxing, this was no ordinary fighter. This was a true potential world champion in the making. After beating Rodrigo Gonzalez by a knockout in three rounds, Lupe Pintor was signed for his first attempt at the World Bantamweight Championship. The attempt was controversial because it brought with it a conflict of interest: the world champion, Carlos Zarate, the man Pintor had to fight to wrest the title, was Lupe's great gymmate and friend. They trained together, ran the roads and talked boxing together. Lupe Pintor had to defeat his best friend to be champ. And he did. Pintor won by a split fifteen-round decision after going to the canvas in round four. Lupe Pintor had become world bantamweight champion.

He was a busy champion. He wanted to fight, he loved fighting, and was getting better and better as experience taught him how to use his supreme God-given talent to the best of his ability. The defence of his new title would begin soon enough. First, there were three non-title bouts. He beat Acencio Melendez by a knockout in the first, avenged his loss to Soto with a ten-round decision win in the second, and lost to Manuel Vasquez by a knockout in six in a rematch fight in the third. After this, he moved on to the defence of his title.

At the first time of asking, on his first title defence, he retained the World Championship with a knockout in 12 rounds over Alberto Sandoval at The Forum in California in front of a huge, mad, bad, adoring crowd of Mexican supporters. He drew the second defence of his title after a 15-round battle with Eijiro Murata in Tokyo.

Each of these boxers would have been a very worthy British,

Commonwealth or European champion. Each of them oozed class, courage and knowledge of their craft. Lupe Pintor proved their equal and their conqueror. He was fast becoming one of the greats of boxing, one of the greats of the bantamweight world. Whoever stepped up to fight him would have to deal with a true professional boxer at his peak and one who was ready for anything. The real Lupe Pintor had arrived. The fast, vicious, arrogant, ruthless champion was waiting for all comers.

On the other side of the Atlantic, Johnny Owen, the Welshman from Merthyr Tydfil, bestrode Europe as its best bantamweight boxer. Throughout the Continent, he had beaten every opponent deemed worthy of the title 'professional boxer' in his weight range. He had proved that he too was an exceptionally gifted and talented fighter. Johnny Owen could do no more than make an appointment with Lupe Pintor to decide who was to be bantamweight world champion; he could do no more than throw down the gauntlet and challenge the world champion. And this he did with true Welsh style and finesse. Lupe Pintor accepted that challenge and invited the Welshman to come and play in his world. Mexico was preparing to take on Wales in a winner-takes-all battle. Wales was confident about returning with the spoils.

Mexico and Wales have much in common. Poverty and a lack of opportunity force the young men of Mexico into the boxing arena, much as they do in the mining valleys of South Wales. Imperialism, and the interference and control of outsiders in affairs of state is something the two countries readily recognise and identify with. The industrial age has left its scars on either side of the Atlantic Ocean and this too resonates with the two nations. The fight between these exceptional men would be a fight of equals. Two rough-and-tough, steely no-nonsense boxers brought up to do what they had to – challenge each other in the boxing ring. Everything either of them had ever done in or out of the fight game throughout their short lifetimes had led to this moment.

Lupe Pintor, a product of the rise from the backstreets of Mexico

City, the Indian from Cuajimalpa, was preparing to defend his World Championship title, and his own personal dream and ambition. His opponent would be Johnny Owen, the Matchstick Man from Merthyr Tydfil, whose stamina, courage and unflappability had turned him from an unknown bantamweight just a few short months previously into a true and worthy challenger on the world stage. The battle was soon to commence. The fight would take place in Los Angeles at the grubby, no-frills Olympic Auditorium in a downtown area known as Little Mexico. There, Lupe Pintor would have the edge.

Lupe Pintor has trained hard to win this fight. So has Johnny Owen.

Lupe Pintor is ready to fight. So is Johnny Owen.

Lupe Pintor looks the part: muscle-toned, sleek, super-fit, arrogant and aggressive. God knows what he will make of the Merthyr Matchstick Man.

Lupe Pintor has risen up from the ranks. So has Johnny Owen.

Lupe Pintor is a worthy champion. Johnny Owen wants that mantle for himself.

16

PRE-FIGHT NIGHT

Johnny Owen will stay with me for ever. Just before the fight, we hugged and wished each other luck. I can't forget his smile. I can't forget his face. I can't forget the way he fought. In the ring, we knew only to fight. Now, I believe he is in my spirit. He is with me, making me stronger, making me a better man.

Lupe Pintor at his home in Mexico City, 2002

Los Angeles is a huge sprawling city on the Pacific Ocean. It is best known for the movie industry and for Hollywood, but it has so much more to offer those who spend the time and energy discovering it. Where else can you go snowboarding in the morning, catch a wave in the afternoon and explore deep into the wilderness, off a busy highway, by evening? There is much more to Los Angeles than meets the eye. The City of Angels has so many faces. Since its time began, this meandering metropolis has inspired legions of dreamers. It is a city forever on the move, always surging forward, with the times and ahead of them. A city that refuses to be defined by a single event, activity or location, but very often defines for us all the word 'modernity'.

Downtown Los Angeles is where the city grew from and nestled in there, among the high-rise skyscraping glass plantations and vibrant ethnic communities that offer exotic shops and restaurants, lies a part of home to a people far from their origins. Little Mexico houses a crowded, hectic immigrant population of legal and illegal communities, all vying for the right to make good in the land of the free. Support for any fellow countryman, any Mexican, trying to box his way to glory here would be substantial, fanatical, maybe even bordering on crazy.

Lupe Pintor was the hero of the people who lived in Little Mexico. More so than any politician or singer or media celebrity, they identified with him. He was the champion of the world after all. And he was *their* champion first and foremost. They were preparing to help and support him, and welcome him home. The champ must win. Whatever his followers could do to make that a reality, they would. Lupe Pintor belonged in Little Mexico. He was one of the people.

Johnny Owen would have had no idea of any of this as he settled in and tried to get some sleep on the jumbo jet flying him across the Atlantic Ocean from London. He wouldn't have had a clue about Los Angeles, except perhaps for what he might have seen on television or read about in travel brochures. For him, one would hazard a guess, Los Angeles was sunshine, clear skies, white beaches and blue seas, with girls free-flowing, stunning and bikini-clad day and night. It's a shame it wasn't that easy. It's a shame there couldn't have been a place like that for Johnny. Reality, as always, lets us all down. Unfortunately for Johnny Owen and all of those about to visit with him, Los Angeles back then was dirty, dangerous, humid, warm, covered in a grey and toxic haze, and coated in a smog that had not been seen in the United Kingdom for decades. Such an environment was not at all ideal for someone used to training in the fresh air of the cold, damp mountains of Wales, or running on the quiet country roads between Merthyr Tydfil and the Brecon Beacons.

Dick Owens must have felt vindicated in delaying their arrival when he first set eyes on the City of Angels. The picture of Los Angeles that greeted the three men from Merthyr Tydfil was pretty uninspiring. It wasn't the best of starts. They wouldn't show their displeasure, though. They would just get on with it, grin and bear it.

Dick Owens, Dai Gardner and Johnny Owen arrived in Los Angeles at around 2.15 p.m. local time on 12 September 1980. They were met by the public relations officer allocated to them for the duration of their stay, Van Barbieu. Van was a gentle, affable professional who had both the success of the promotion and the welfare of both boxers at heart (an extremely delicate balancing act). The men were whisked off to the Gala Motor Hotel in downtown Los Angeles, their place of abode for the duration of their stay. The first duty for Johnny Owen was that he should attend a press conference. The media were eager, ready and waiting to meet the bantamweight challenger from Merthyr Tydfil.

His requested attendance at this, his first media gathering in the United States, had been preying on his mind ever since he had been made aware of it. Johnny Owen hated this sort of thing. He despised the rigmarole, the commercialism and the selling of tickets. Like the true professional that he was, he understood that it had to happen and so he got on with it. As it turned out, the experience was not an unpleasant one. It was quite laid back and surprised not just Johnny but all of them. They had expected a more confrontational question-and-answer time. Maybe that would come later.

The press conference took place at around five o'clock in the afternoon. They chatted a bit, answered what they could, parried what they were able to and Dai Gardner fended off one or two of the more confusing media assumptions (they were all still disorientated after the flight). As soon as it was over, they were free to go, to do whatever they wanted, relax and prepare. After a light meal, they went back to the hotel where Johnny and Dick, father and son, shared a room together. Dai Gardner's room was next door. The boxer and the trainer had an early night. They had worked out a schedule in advance which dictated that they go to bed early in order to recover and readjust after the 12-hour flight. It was Dick's plan that their bodies and minds should get onto Los Angeles time as quickly as possible and acclimatise to the conditions at every opportunity.

Everyone assumed that they would be allowed to rest and recuperate in peace. In theory, that seemed a perfectly understandable assumption, but the media gremlins had not finished with them yet, and when the trainer and the boxer tried to settle down for the evening they were interrupted by the fanatical, over-excited Mexican press corps almost continuously. The telephone would not stop ringing. Dick quickly became alert to the seriousness of the problem. He was furious too and asked Dai Gardner to do something to stop the phone calls getting into the room. Johnny had to have a near-perfect preparation in order to have any chance of beating Lupe Pintor. They both knew that. As grateful as they were for the interest from the press, no intrusion must be allowed to upset their long-established plan. Dai Gardner took the matter up with the hotel management and the calls stopped. The beginning of the intrusion into their lives had begun, though, and it would not end so easily the next time. This was big-time boxing and Johnny was hot property.

Johnny slept for 14 hours straight that night and suffered little or no jet lag upon awakening. In fact, he seemed so refreshed he wanted to fight Lupe Pintor that very Friday night instead of hanging around in Los Angeles for another week. Things were beginning to feel better all round.

During their first day in California, they wallowed in 80 degree heat and were near-smothered in the humid atmosphere. Johnny and his manager spent the day going through tiresome medical examinations, eye tests and form-filling – it took five hours to clear the red tape. The Californian Boxing Commission was very thorough – they seemed to want to know everything about the boxer from Wales. Johnny was glad when it was all over. His training schedule began in earnest the very next day.

He began, as he would begin on every other morning leading up to the fight, with a long and exhausting eight-and-a-half-mile run in the local park. Sometimes, he would meet Lupe Pintor running in the opposite direction, towards him. Not once did the two men acknowledge each other. Johnny was surprised at the champ's height. Pintor was only 5 ft 4 in. tall; shorter than Johnny had thought. It was not lost on the challenger that he had a good height advantage. This was an important discovery. Johnny had discovered an edge, an angle, a psychological one maybe, but they all count.

Johnny Owen was allocated a minder and a driver for these trips to the park. Johnny Carbrerra was a big and burly professional assistant from good Italian stock. His job was to stick with the Merthyr Tydfil boxer each morning and afternoon, to look after him and ensure he got to his training assignments. Almost all of these were beyond walking distance and he needed a car to get to them. It was not an option to run or walk to the park or to the gym or whatever. This was Los Angeles for a start and could be dangerous for a stranger alone. The security implications were obvious. Johnny Owen was glad of the minder. The two men got on well.

Johnny Carbrerra had seen all kinds of boxers come and go over the years, and had looked after many of them. He was the ultimate professional and his words of experience have meaning and resonance. He had never seen a boxer that looked quite like Johnny. When he first set eyes on his skeletal body, he felt he should not be anywhere near a boxing ring. But his opinion was to change drastically over the period he worked with the Welshman. To this day, he maintains that the fitness Johnny Owen displayed on those early-morning runs remains unique to him. He would always remember Johnny Owen.

After roadwork, when the run was completed, Carbrerra would take Johnny to the gym. The Welshman's afternoon was then spent shadow boxing, working with pads and the jump rope, and doing benchwork. Sometimes, he would pound the heavy bag, hour after hour, sweat pouring from his brow, arms flailing. There would be no saunas and no sparring. They did not want to expose Johnny's style to Lupe Pintor or in any way soften him up before the fight.

After the training was done, they had the rest of the day off to do as they wished. The Gala Motor Hotel was not the finest abode Los Angeles had to offer. It was based in the Mexican quarter, there were bars on the windows and the walk to it from the road was not pleasant. Still, there was a swimming-pool and, nine times out of ten, they would relax, have a meal and sit by the pool. Sometimes, they'd walk around the city to take in the atmosphere and sights of downtown Los Angeles, and get a breath of the air in Little Mexico. In truth, they were bored stiff. Johnny wanted to go to Disneyland, to have a look at the place (it fascinated him) and have some fun. There was no time. It was something they thought to do after the fight, perhaps.

The boredom, though, had its advantages. It forced them to think more deeply about the coming battle with Lupe Pintor and eased them into harder work. They also had to deal with the usual publicity surrounding a World Championship fight. The press and media were never too far away. Whether they liked it or not, the celebrity side of things had to be faced. However, the Mexican journalists had begun to worry Johnny. They were acting quite differently from the rest of the media. They had begun to hound the Merthyr Tydfil man more than was necessary and their behaviour was to eventually cause major problems for the Owen camp.

Johnny was pursued all week by reporters, photographers and TV crews, most of Mexican origin. As soon he began his run in the morning, they were there. In the afternoon, at the Los Angeles Sports Arena, the training gym both boxers were using for the fight, it was the same. Johnny altered his training schedule, delayed gym work and stormed off when they found him again or caught on to his whereabouts. They would not leave him alone. The Owen camp thought that the whole thing with the Mexican press was orchestrated. They felt Lupe Pintor's team was behind it all. That the assaults on Johnny's peace and privacy were a deliberate attempt to disrupt his preparation and undermine him. The normally placid Johnny finally lost his cool and threatened to change hotels and disrupt the whole of the promoters' plans, saying that it had been a mistake to allow the promoters to book them into a hotel in the Mexican quarter in the first place. Everyone agreed with him. Johnny shouted loud enough and things were eventually smoothed over. Someone called off the media dogs. The experience was not one that would be recalled with fondness.

Dai Gardner wanted Johnny Owen to spar at the Olympic Auditorium (the venue for the upcoming battle with Lupe Pintor) in public, as part of a television interview. Johnny was none too amused.

He didn't fancy participating in either. He wasn't a public kind of person. The world of celebrity didn't really suit the young Merthyr man. He wasted no time in telling his manager 'no dice'. He wouldn't publicly present himself anywhere for anyone. Dick, realising Johnny would have to do something for the fight promotion and do it in the way the Americans wanted, donned the mantle of father as well as trainer and mediated between Dai and Van Barbieu, the public relations officer for the fight.

Barbieu offered to vet the sparring partners for Johnny. He also offered to organise the press conference in such a way as to allow Johnny to answer set questions instead of making statements or speeches. A compromise was quickly reached. After much persuasion, Johnny Owen agreed to take part.

On 16 September 1980, Johnny Owen stood before the television cameras, fending off the questions of the press. The conference took place at the Brown Derby Hotel in Hollywood. The chandeliers were bigger than the boxer's front room. His legs sank up to his knees in the carpets whilst he ate. Gathered before him that morning, the international back-page press. Also there in force were the rich and the not so rich; the famous and the infamous; and boxers and those to do with boxing, and the fight promotion. Johnny began well. He explained that he came from Merthyr Tydfil, an industrial iron and coal town in South Wales in the United Kingdom. Most of those gathered hadn't a clue where Merthyr Tydfil was geographically. Some didn't even know where Wales was. Johnny tried to explain to them that Merthyr Tydfil was in Wales, which was next door to England, which was next door to Europe – the Continent of which he was champion. No one ever really knew whether Johnny's geography lesson worked or not. There were a lot of vague-looking faces gazing up at him from the audience, that was for sure.

A question was asked about his looks. 'You don't look like a boxer, you have no marks, no cuts! What's the story? Why is that?'

Johnny, in a dry and sarcastic moment, replied, 'The promoters don't pay me enough to get marked.' They enjoyed that, then asked about his ambitions. 'My ambition is to win the world title.'

'Do you have another ambition?' someone shouted from the back. 'Something more personal perhaps?'

He paused and looked round the room reflecting on the opulence and eyeing up the privileged few gathered before him, the crystal chandeliers, the thick-pile carpet and the perfectly set tables.

'Yes,' he said at last. 'I'd like a hotel like this back home in Merthyr Tydfil for my mother and father and brothers and sisters.' Everyone loved the answer. It was refreshing to all gathered there to actually hear someone speak truthfully about ambitions that had some meaning. They could relate to Johnny Owen. Everyone could. The young boxer, from somewhere most of them hadn't a clue about, had firmly placed the press on his side. At least for now. But Johnny meant what he said. To own and run a hotel was what he wanted. It was a wonderful ambition. That answer ended the press conference. Johnny Owen had done remarkably well.

When the tickets eventually went on sale, the first 40 were snapped up by a lady with a Welsh accent. She would be the first of many to visit Los Angeles from Wales that week. The invasion of Johnny Owen supporters, although never going to be large in number, had begun.

Lupe Pintor, Johnny Owen and their handlers, trainers and managers all lived in close proximity to one another, and would see each other at close quarters almost daily. Pintor was staying in the next hotel to Johnny's. The two camps and the hotels shared the large swimming-pool. The differences between the two fighters were highlighted for all to see during their sessions of relaxation at either end of the pool. The differences were quite extraordinary.

Pintor looked immensely strong and muscular. When Johnny stripped off at the pool to sunbathe, Pintor's handlers couldn't get over how thin he was. They were astonished. They sniggered and laughed at the Welshman. They gave him their own nickname, 'the Bionic Bantam'. Johnny secretly vowed to silence them. What astonished the Owen camp about Pintor was his eating habits. Johnny would eat salads and steaks, whilst his adversary tucked into pancakes smothered in syrup. He didn't put weight on, though, and hadn't had a weight problem in any of his 47 fights, 42 of which he'd won, 35 inside the distance. He was a formidable opponent indeed and one to be respected regardless of what he ate.

Many Johnny Owen fans had made the long and arduous trip from Wales to support their hero. Merthyr Tydfil to Los Angeles is an awful long way to come to watch a boxing match. They could not match the Mexicans in their support, but they were enthusiastic and of good cheer, and they were in Los Angeles to do their damnedest for their man Johnny. They would support him to the hilt.

Dick, indeed most of the Owen camp, felt it their duty to take time out to be with these supporters whenever they had an opportunity. Dick especially enjoyed a pleasant evening the night before the fight discussing the pros and cons of the coming world title battle with his countrymen. It was an honour for him to be among them. He hoped his son would do them proud. He knew his son would do them proud. Their support was so very welcome.

One can only imagine what it must have been like the night before the fight for those in the Owen camp. This was the end of the dream for them all and very soon they would know how it was to turn out. Nerves must have been jangling that evening before the battle of Little Mexico. The questions and the doubts would be a part of the thinking leading up to the sound of the first bell. Were they too far from home? Had they travelled too far, too quickly? How could they possibly win in this Mexican stronghold? What would be the price of such a victory? No matter what you gain in life, there is always a price to pay. The problem is we rarely know the price until later. There are a thousand maybes and what ifs that go through the minds of those closely concerned with a major event such as this. One thing was for sure, Johnny Owen was here at the crossroads; he had arrived at the very heart of his dream, a dream he had harboured all these years. It was time to face destiny. And that can be a very scary place to be.

Johnny Owen was indeed a long way from home. To him, it was cold of spirit here in Los Angeles: foreign, lonely and cold. Coming from a close-knit community like Merthyr Tydfil, it must have seemed very strange indeed for all those concerned to be in a place of almost pure business values. Life was much better in Merthyr Tydfil than anything any of them had seen in Los Angeles. That was for sure. And there were dangers here. There was street violence and muggings and they were aware of store robberies and of guns going off. These were dangers none of them had come across before. Dick especially felt very insecure on that last pre-fight night. Lying in the darkness of his hotel room awaiting sleep, he must have wondered if his son felt that way, too.

Soon, they would all be asleep, dreaming of World Championship glory. The day of the fight was upon them.

17

FIGHT NIGHT

Bankers, financiers, lawyers and clerks; politicians, teachers, dentists and show business 'celebrities'; golfers, doctors, accountants and pressmen; vicars and bishops of all God's holy churches; and an odour and vacuous hint of royalty, steeped in the traditions of mayhem and theft, to top off the fare. Fat cats with thin cigars, thick cats with fat cigars, heartless tight-lipped skinny cats desperately holding onto the very air that they breathe and non-smokers, just in case. Yes! All are alive and well, and they are all here! All here to pay their due respect to those with courage to spare and share, to those with an idea of what life really is about and a plan for where they are to go. They are here to respect and pray. Pray their kids will follow their lead and never wind up in this mess of trouble. Pray that they will never see the hard times that turn any of them or their offspring into barbaric ring fighters. They settle themselves, light a cigar, place a bet, crack a joke with their neighbour, pretend they are 'men' and prepare to watch the fight of all fights, or as the bill so hyperbolically spells out to the childlike and infantile mind, this is the fight of the century.

It was the day of the fight. It was warm and dry, and on the surface no different from the day before. The hot sun was fighting to break through the manmade haze and smog which emanated from the non-stop traffic racing up and down the jam-packed eight-lane freeway. Everything was normal and everyone was tending to business, like the day before. It was just another day in LA. For some, though, it was *the* day. A day prepared for and dreamed of for so long. All the hard work, all the running and training, all those hard-fought battles in and out of the ring, all the endless hours of meticulous preparation – all would be resolved this day and their worth known. This was World Championship fight day. It didn't get any bigger or better than that, not for any boxer and certainly not for the boxers' entourages.

In Lupe Pintor's camp, they awoke and went about the slow and determined business of pre-fight preparation. Check the fighter, check the gear and check the crew. Check the food, check the weight and check the clothing. Check the hotel and check the flights out. And that was just for starters. The rituals were all adhered to, the superstitions and religious connotations abided by, the mundane and regular functions of life performed as if it was just another day. It was a scenario played out before every fight and by every boxer. This fight day was a little bit special, though. This was a World Championship fight and no one, not even the very laid-back employee working in the vicinity of the bout, on its very fringes, could fail to feel the excitement or capture the tingling apprehension thrown up by the atmosphere. This was the ultimate contest between two men, the absolute examination – sport's greatest test.

Johnny Owen, his trainer and his manager left for the weigh-in at the Olympic Auditorium in the late morning. Johnny had no weight problem. Not this time. He chatted casually to two big, interested Americans as he waited for the observers, officials and the media to deal with whatever else there was to be dealt with. The bureaucracy and publicity seemed never ending. The two American men appeared to be working for security. They were awaiting their instructions for the night ahead. They wished the Merthyr Tydfil boxer the very best of luck. Johnny thanked them kindly.

Before the American pair were engaged in their duties, they both passed on a little advice to Johnny's manager. If Johnny were to win the fight tonight, they said, it might be a good idea if he and the Owen camp were to make their way to the airport immediately and catch the first plane home and out of Los Angeles. Get back to London as quickly as you can, was their advice. It might not be too safe around the stadium if Lupe Pintor were to be defeated. His fans would be everywhere and they would be as mad as hell. For the duration of the fight, and in the close vicinity of the Olympic Auditorium, they should remember one thing – to all intents and purposes, they are in Mexico. For tonight, it is Mexico. They shouldn't think for one minute they are in the United States. Dai and Johnny listened intently to the advice. They thanked the two men and moved on.

The Olympic Auditorium holds 10,000 people. That night, as expected, the house was full. Full beyond capacity and probably dangerously so. Most of the mad, cheering mass of spectators were Mexican – of Mexican Indian descent in all probability – here only to cheer on El Indio de Cuajimalpa – Lupe Pintor. The Welsh were outnumbered by 100 to 1 at least in the vast indoor stadium. Even so, they sang and cheered, and they had a great time in doing so. For now, the Mexicans, believing their man to be invincible, left the contingent of supporters from Wales alone. They patronised them and put up with them, for now.

Around the ring itself, patiently awaiting Lupe Pintor and Johnny Owen, sat sports reporters and television people, the judges, cameras and cameramen, officials and doctors, and all those with business in the fight game. Behind them was an alleyway for all to pass and walk freely, and bordering that walkway sat the lucky ones, the ringside-seat ticket holders. Above the elite and directly above the ring itself, the bright white halogen light that affects the theatre of boxing so very deeply. Streams of grey-blue smoke coiled to the heavens in ephemeral criss-cross rivers. An atmosphere of childlike illegality and anticipation filled the air. Everyone waited with bated breath for the champion and his principal contender to appear.

The Olympic Auditorium had become a hostile, sweltering cauldron. The crowd seemed intimidating and dangerous. They were building themselves up into a frenzy in anticipation of Lupe Pintor's appearance. At the top of their voices they screamed and shouted, 'Lupe! Lupe! Lupe! Lupe! LUPE! LUPE! LUPE!'

In Wales, Johnny's supporters sat around radios and waited at telephones for news of the fight. Johnny's mother, Edith, always anxious when her son fought, could do nothing more than wait. She knew what to do and when. She would telephone Dai Gardner's wife or the press at Thompson House for the result when the time came. In the meantime, she'd do something else to keep herself busy and try to take her mind off everything.

Many had predicted there'd be a bad night ahead for Johnny Owen. He was fighting a hard man in a hard place and now those around him began to realise what that meant. The American professional watchers were getting edgy. They had never seen Johnny fight. They had never given him anything much by way of credit since he had flown to Los Angeles a full week ago. The TV men said he looked ridiculous, that he was out of his depth. They believed he would last a round or two and then he'd be off home. Lupe Pintor was not just loved by Mexicans, he was admired by boxing fans everywhere and those fans could not see a way that Johnny Owen could even trouble Pintor.

In Johnny's dressing-room, the talking had stopped. The waiting was over. Immediate pre-fight planning had taken precedence. All they could hear from the auditorium above was the sound of the Mexican fans shouting for their man. 'LUPE! LUPE! LUPE!' On and on it went. It became their backing track. It became the music they thought to. They got used to it eventually. Ignored it. It didn't silence them, they kept talking, but they were always very aware of it.

Dick Owens was there, as was Dai Gardner, along with two other unsung heroes, the cornermen, Ken Bryant and Nat Nicholls, essential elements in the planning. Without their expertise, nothing much would go right during the fight itself. Their job would be pivotal to the smooth running of operations between rounds.

Dick and Dai, attempting to quell nerves, were busy giving their man all the last-minute advice they felt he needed. They went over all the instructions again and again. Tactics that had been thought through long and hard were repeated, dissected and assessed for the battle ahead. Everything that Johnny Owen needed to be in the ring with him was checked and double-checked, and sometimes triple-checked. Dick and Dai occasionally paced a little worry out of their systems, but all in all it was calm.

It seemed Johnny's professional entourage felt the tension more than Johnny himself. Perhaps the Matchstick Man had a plan of his own. He seemed assured, unruffled and tranquil. He seemed confident. This was his day and no one was going to snatch it away from him. Not even the tough Mexican fighter he was about to come up against. Johnny Owen was ready to rock 'n' roll. Johnny Owen was ready to be crowned bantamweight champion of the world.

'The quiet man', as Dick liked to sometimes call him, was taking it all very well indeed. Here was a young man with courage and dignity, willingly holding the hopes and dreams of so many on his thin and seemingly brittle shoulders as he readied himself for the battle ahead. On the walk to the ring, Johnny was reminded time and again of the tactics. He was to attack Pintor from the word go, keep his hands up high so that the Mexican would punch to the body only, keep Pintor close, shut down the ring, make his footwork count against him and press forward all the time. All the time, press forward. That was important.

Pintor must be made aware of his opponent's stamina early on. That alone would make him think. If you cannot tire an opponent and you've got no room to hit him as you wish, and he keeps coming at you for round after round after round, you are bound to lose heart. Johnny Owen was after Lupe Pintor's heart tonight, and his spirit. He wanted to defeat his soul. It was a plan he hoped would work. All he could do from within himself now was to hope and maybe pray a little. From without, all Johnny had to do was to face the fans. The fans that filled the stadium with the terrifying cry of 'LUPE! LUPE! LUPE!' The Welsh supporters were still vastly outnumbered. It would be a difficult night for them as they tried to be heard in the crowd. But still they sang.

As they climbed the stairs to their destiny – Johnny Owen, Dick,

Dai and the two cornermen – many of the spectators close to them began wilfully pushing and pinching the Welsh champion. The Mexican fans' attitude to the challenger bordered on a frenzy of hatred that would have intimidated most fighters immediately. Johnny's team showed concern all right, but their man was cool, calm and collected. Like someone who had an inner knowledge and a peace within, he seemed immune to it all. When they reached the top of the stairs, he held his arms up high in the air. Then, as though to confound those who sought to bring fear into his heart, Johnny Owen bounced into the arena as though the ardent Mexican Lupe Pintor fans were shouting his praises. It was a performance of high quality and real courage. If it gained him little respect with the Mexican fans, it earned him much respect with the media and with Pintor himself. 'Johnny had no nerves at all and I was a very proud man,' Dick reflected some time later.

Without the red-for-Wales dressing gown with the Matchstick Man logo on his back, Johnny looked fragile and frail in the ring. To those who had not seen him before in shorts and ready to box, it was a shock. To those close to him, who knew how fit and strong he was, he looked in peak condition. Lupe Pintor arrived to an ovation and, after acknowledging his supporters with a wave of both hands and a short walk around the ring, he stared ominously at his opponent. Pintor, short, squat and with the promise of violence in every movement and all around him looked like a world champion should look.

When not in the ring, the referee, a top-class pro called Marty Denkin, was a federal investigator for the US Equal Employment Commission. He was a no-nonsense tough cookie who advocated fair play and the game played by the rules. He was a hugely respected arbitrator.

'LUPE! LUPE! LUPE!' the chanting continued. No eye contact was made between the two boxers. The referee read both their rights and the rules, and possibly the riot act. There was no going back now. For both boxers, the adrenalin would have been rushing around the body, preparing them, hyping them up. They returned to their allocated, independent corners and waited. The crowd continued to scream and shout throughout. Pintor crossed himself and delivered a short prayer. Johnny tapped his gloves together, once, twice, and looked to the ground, maybe praying also. Still no eye contact was made between the two boxers.

The sound of the bell smashed the world into a different dimension. The fight was under way. The waiting was over.

Round one was hard fought and almost even, with Johnny relentlessly pushing forward, going after Pintor and stunning his critics in his pursuit of the champion from the first sound of the bell. It was crystal clear that the Welshman had come here to attack the Mexican. Owen was looking like a fighter who expected to win. He looked like a fighter who had no fear of Lupe Pintor. In the end, Johnny may well have edged the round. He certainly surprised the champ with style, technique and courage. The first psychological battle had been won by the man from Merthyr Tydfil.

Rounds two and three both went to the Welshman, but Lupe Pintor's right-hooks and uppercuts were beginning to intervene, halting Johnny Owen's progress in the mean time. The challenger continued to attack nonetheless, but supporters and friends of the champion were starting to take note of his intentions. The Mexican was beginning to wake up. He had become alert to the genuine challenge Owen presented. The Welshman's philosophy seemed to be the best form of defence is attack.

The fourth round was even. Although, Pintor's right-hand struck with force. Those close to it felt it. Those watching on TV would not have known. One cannot really imagine the impact by way of television. Johnny weathered it. He came out of it fine. He was dominating the fight at this stage. Pintor had become subdued and puzzled. It should have been easy and all over by now. The champion wasn't sure what was happening. It was not going to script for the Mexican.

In the fifth, Johnny started to bleed badly and began to swallow blood from a huge laceration to the inside of his bottom lip. Both the doctor and Marty Denkin, the referee, tracked him closely from then on. They would make sure he was OK and not weakened or affected dangerously by the blood loss. The truth was, at this stage, that both men were cut badly. The fifth round had been important. It had tired them both. Nothing is so unbelievably long as a fiercely contested three-minute round. The fifth had been such a round.

Still, the Welshman came relentlessly forward in the sixth, refusing to give Pintor the chances he needed to do the things he wanted to do. Johnny was spoiling, and spoiling well. The champion must have wondered when he was going to back off and leave him alone. Johnny Owen's bravery astonished all that watched, including Pintor's most rabid supporters.

The seventh and eighth were edged by Lupe, but he still couldn't shake off the Welshman. In the ninth, the Mexican changed his style. He had recognised that he was in serious trouble, so he gambled and left space. Then he stepped back and gave himself room to punch, and punch he did. He knocked Johnny Owen to the floor. The challenger was up in an instant. The referee asked if he was OK and checked his eyes. It seemed he was. Johnny fought on.

The change in Pintor's game plan, the knock-down and the loss of blood from the cut to the Welshman's lip wound were beginning to tell. Johnny Owen was running out of steam. His heart kept him in this race, and his courage and stubbornness, so often his secret weapons in tight corners, now became his secret adversaries. He fought a great tenth round, but in the eleventh seemed to be exhausted almost beyond recovery. Marty Denkin felt it should be over, but the challenger's corner said no and Johnny miraculously recovered to battle on.

Out he came for the 12th and he was knocked down again. But he got up to continue, yet again. The courage of the Welshman was all the commentators could talk about. Even though all looked lost, they hailed the man from Merthyr Tydfil. He had shown them. But the crowd was going mad for Pintor. 'LUPE! LUPE! LUPE! LUPE!' The noise was deafening. Things were being thrown into the ring. It was a sign of what was to come. Soon, it would be over.

From somewhere, Pintor found a new lease of life and Johnny Owen was knocked to the floor by one of the most vicious right-hand punches ever witnessed anywhere. He was rendered unconscious before he hit the canvas. The crowd of mainly Mexican supporters went crazy with joy.

Johnny lay there on the ground not responding to salts or oxygen or kind words. Confusion reigned supreme. Dai Gardner looked shocked beyond words. Dick Owens cried from the bottom of his soul. Unconscious still, Johnny was removed on a stretcher from the ring. He was carried head high almost, through the badly behaved baying mob of Mexican so-called boxing fans and eventually taken by ambulance to the nearest available hospital.

18

GLADIATORS (3)

God has ordered us to treat the Holy Spirit, in as much as it is tender and delicate, in accordance with the good of its own nature, with tranquillity and gentleness and quiet and peace, not to disturb it with madness, rage, anger and grief.

The pain had been instant. Instant, gut-wrenching and indescribable. The world had changed. Everything had tumbled out of sync. This was fairy-tale land gone wrong, gone upside down. This was the black side of doom. In one nanosecond of unbelievable ferocity and bad fortune, something so awful had befallen the world that he was too shaken to even begin to describe it. It seemed as though it was just not true. It was unbelievable and his life had incalculably and irredeemably been snatched away from him. Everything he had worked for, fought for all these years, prayed to come to fruition, had been snatched away. Everything he held so dear, so close, and his loving, wonderful, tender, smiling Johnny had been taken from him. He needed to think. He was desperate to think, desperate to clear his mind. He took a big deep breath and in that breath the questions of philosophy rose to the surface and from somewhere deep within the telling began.

How can one not know how valuable things are until they are gone?

Why do we human beings think that material things mean anything at all? Why do we think there is any solace of any kind in wealth? We already have wealth. It is in our sons and our daughters, in our lands and our culture, in our hearts and minds, in our health and in our acceptance of death. That is where true wealth lies. And when what we really need is cruelly taken from us and we are allowed to see it for what it is, it makes us weep because we should have been able to see it all along. We should have known better. It pains us to understand that we were so wrong about the world.

He felt now as though he had been lying to himself all along, that he had conned himself. He felt he was going to die. It was all his fault. He was to blame. No one could ever take that blame away from him. *No one! Not ever!* He wouldn't let them.

The boxing ring was empty. Only the ghosts of boxers long gone fought there now. He stood, staring at the bare barren canvas, pondering the rope that held the game in place. He stood in the shadows of the gloom, in deep profound silence. Everything looked so different now, everything more real. The bell seemed more officious than it had ever done, the judges' table was more rational, more wise, and the light above the boxing ring itself insightful and full of knowledge. What had really taken place here in the name of sport on this dark, black night? It was too soon to answer that one.

One thing he did know for certain was that if anything happened to Johnny, he'd give it up. Give it all up. He'd never go near a boxing ring again. It wasn't worth it any more. Johnny meant everything to him. More than any of this fight business ever would. He'd be unable to go on. Not any more, not like this, not if anything should happen. How could he?

Then he began to replay the fight in his head, in his mind.

What happened? What happened? What happened?

One minute, it was exciting and nail-biting and loud and full of hope; the next, it was nothing, hopeless and empty. One minute, they were on top of the world. They were winning and readying for home, and the adulation and acceptance of the crowds of well-wishing fans that would surely have come out to greet and crown their new hero and champion. The next minute, they were at the bottom of the well with nowhere to go. How do you come to terms with that?

It had happened so quickly, in a nanosecond. Johnny didn't see it. He couldn't have because when the punch landed, it was all over. He knew. He knew before Johnny had hit the canvas. Everyone knew the great man, the wonderful courageous fighter, was in trouble. No one there could have failed to notice.

It was time to go and help him now. First, he would pray. He hadn't prayed in years, but he would now.

Please God, make him OK, make our Johnny OK.

Come to think of it, he had seen the punch coming, but not here, not now and not then. From way back, it came. It was as though he'd seen it before, in a dream or somewhere. It was as if he'd been expecting it. He shivered. Life is strange. It wasn't of this world, but of another and, like some tormenting action replay, it had been shown to him once again, this time in real life. He looked around. He had no idea where he was now or what he should do. Frightened, lonely and desperate, he wanted it all to be right again. He wiped away tears. They were supposed to be tears of joy tonight, that was how it was supposed to end. A gun had gone off in his head when the punch landed. And here he was, suddenly old and frail, feeling hopelessly inadequate, sitting in an ambulance, racing to a hospital on the other side of the world.

God, please save us all! Please!

Deep down, he knew that this prayer would not be heeded or, if it were, it would be heeded in a very different way from the way he wished it. Often that is the case. We think something bad has happened only to see something good come from it. But what good could come of this?

Please God, save us all! Please!

He knew it was all over and all was lost, so he wept again. His pain – too deep, too unbearable to deal with – could only be assuaged by tears. The ambulance sped on through downtown LA, through the mad streets of a country with no shame. He tried to figure it out yet again.

What happened? What happened? What the hell happened?

All he knew was they were winning. They were miles ahead and no question. Everyone knew it. Ready to board the plane with the belt, they were. All those lovely dreams they talked about for so long into the night were about to come right. Merthyr Tydfil would have been proud. The people of Merthyr Tydfil would have been proud whatever happened, but they would have been prouder with victory.

Why didn't Johnny see it? Was he so tired, so unaware? Had they made a mistake, to be here in the first place, here in this God-forsaken haven of Mammon?

Johnny had held his own against the champion, no one could argue with that and he was in the lead. Being in the lead, though, is always a dangerous place to be. No matter what the sport. The opponent will always fight hard when behind. There was no argument, though. He had been in the lead, till the ninth. He was not taking a beating even then. Even when the champion came at him and caught him and slowed him down. If he had been taking a beating, they'd have stopped it. That first right to the head in the 12th round, even that was OK. The referee had said so. He had asked if Johnny wanted to go on. He wasn't hurt. Not right then, not at that point.

Lupe Pintor had been favourite to win, they knew that, but he brought no new battle plan to the fight. A good left-hook and lots of courage had made Pintor what he was, so he needed no new battle plan. He was confident. They knew what the champion was going to do, they knew he'd be overconfident perhaps, they knew what he was going to fight like from the start. His stamina puzzled them, though. Pintor had more left in the tank towards the end. They'd never have guessed that.

Johnny knew before he started that the champion's punches would catch him. He'd worked on that possibility. He had to. Pintor was a world champion after all. You don't get to be world champion without being a bit special. So getting clipped by Pintor was taken on board and worked out in training. Johnny himself had thought out how to handle the punches. But no one could ever know how much those clips would take out of him.

So, it must have been stamina. Of all the things they didn't allow for, stamina was the last thing they thought would beat him. He pondered that and then dismissed it as he continued the action replay of the fight.

Johnny had shown them. Shown them that, despite his ghostly pale and thin frame, he was a true champion. At times, he clearly outboxed Pintor, not hitting him with anything hard, but cutting the champion in the third and fourth rounds over both eyes. Pintor was shocked all right. All the way up until the punch landed he'd been shocked. In the end, he took little notice as Johnny was taken from the ring on the stretcher. Perhaps he was able to come to terms with it. Maybe he couldn't look. Maybe one day he would ask him.

The crowd was appalling. Fans of the champion showed no respect. It was beyond intimidating, beyond dangerous in the ring, with the broken boxer waiting to be treated. The crowd was out of control, throwing stuff at a sick man and those who sought to help him. They continued to bay for his demise, attacking and robbing those who helped Johnny to the ambulance. They were appalling. The champion had gone to celebrate when Johnny was taken to the California Hospital Medical Center. The doctors removed a blood clot. It took over three hours. The operation had saved his life. And then they waited. Waited for God to decide their fates. And when those fates were decided they would have to make sense of them.

Why doesn't life get easier? Why is it always a struggle? Why is there no respite? Why do we have to box? What is the point?

If they hadn't lived where they'd lived, then perhaps boxing wouldn't have been what they did. Maybe they'd have done something else. He was tired now. Tired, emotionally and physically, but still he wanted to walk. So he walked.

He walked and walked and walked and walked and finally he paused. He was in a strange place, he knew that, and he could sense danger but he paused nonetheless. He paused when he heard something he thought he'd recognised, in a building close by. So he went to the sound and looked into the building. Through the tears streaming down his cheeks, through the window of a dark and dowdy bar-room, he glimpsed a TV set. Black and white pictures of two boxers, both black, slugging it out in some long-forgotten fight, were entertaining the drunk and the not-so-drunk. From within the bar, they cheered as first one fighter struck and then the other fought back. Then everyone gathered in the bar-room laughed as one boxer took a beating and was floored to the canvas.

As he watched, through the mist of his sorrow, the word gladiator came to him.

That's what they were! Modern-day gladiators!

He grasped the possibility and somehow it cheered him a little, but not much. Not much because he was desperately worried and desperately sad for Johnny.

Two policemen came and stood with him, and he talked with them for a while and in the end they helped him home.

Gladiators! He told them. Gladiators! I've seen them. Just now! On the TV!

19

AFTER THE GOLD RUSH

Early snows settled up top, on the Merthyr Tydfil hills, like a shroud. The valley dressed proper for sadness. Johnny had come home the day before. Driven through Rhymney and Tredegar, and over Dowlais, finally resting in the old church at the foot of the town. Merthyr had prepared for mourning well. Tragedy comes naturally here. It's almost expected. It knew instinctively how to respond. 'This is a tough town,' said an old man. 'People become hard here because they have to be.'

Johnny Owen lay asleep in a deep coma. He was under the care of the highly qualified medical staff at the Lutheran Hospital on Hope Street in downtown Los Angeles. In the 24 hours since his admission, the hospital had received over 100 calls and telegrams from all over the world wishing the young boxer well. The official hospital statement delivered the next morning was clinical and emotion-free, as most official statements on health generally are, and stated: 'Johnny Owen was brought to the emergency department on Friday, 19 September 1980 in a critical condition. He was operated on for a blood clot on the brain between 11.30 p.m. and 3.30 a.m. Mr Owen remains in a critical condition and will remain so for the next 72 hours.'

Dick Owens was suffering badly. He had been too distraught to think or do much of anything since the fight. He was lost. There was talk of Edith coming over to Los Angeles to be with him, but he wasn't sure whether or not his wife should make the trip. He instinctively felt that it would be better for her to stay at home and wait for Johnny to return. His arguments made for good theory, but it wasn't to be. Edith had a mind of her own and was determined to be with both her son and her husband in their hour of need. On Sunday, 21 September 1980, two days after Johnny Owen had fought Lupe Pintor for the Bantamweight Championship of the World, Edith Owens arrived at her son's bedside. Emergency travel arrangements had been put into place for her by the Foreign Office back home in Britain and the American Embassy in Washington. She must have hoped the sound of her voice would bring Johnny round, that her presence would trigger a recovery. She was distraught and just wanted to be there. On the Sunday evening, Dick and Edith were reunited with their son. They cried for most of the night.

On Monday morning, they were both taken to the Gala Motor Hotel to meet Dai Gardner. The meeting was pumped full of emotion. When it was over, they all went to the hospital where they met with John Holly, the neurosurgeon in charge of Johnny's care. The doctor asked Dick how many fights his son had fought in. He told him 124 as an amateur and 28 as a professional. The doctor went on to tell them what he felt had happened to Johnny. What, in his opinion, had occurred to cause his present condition. After a thorough examination and an X-ray along with many other independent tests, he could now more or less tell what had gone wrong.

Johnny Owen had been born with an unseen physical deformity. He had an inordinately strong jaw and a wafer-thin skull. Instead of the jawbone breaking on the impact of Pintor's right-hand punch, it crashed straight through into the thinner skull. Lupe Pintor's punch had literally forced Johnny's jawbone into his brain, causing him irreparable damage. It could have happened at any time, in any fight, even perhaps in any other situation not related to boxing.

Dick and Edith, like everyone else involved, were stunned by the news. Dick was especially downcast. If only they'd known, they would have put all their efforts into running. Johnny would never have boxed. They couldn't dwell on the past and worry about what ifs, though. They had to deal with the present and take each day as it came. The first thing they had to do was accept Johnny's condition. The medical implications were now obvious. Johnny's life was in the balance. It was touch-and-go. He had to fight like never before to survive. Soon after the meeting with John Holly, Johnny underwent another operation on his brain. The procedure was to relieve pressure caused by the swelling of the head. The operation went ahead quickly, as soon as permission had been given to the hospital. It was successful. Despite that success, Johnny Owen contracted pneumonia, a further complication. Modern drugs and well-established treatments quickly cleared the problem, but it had been a tricky time and gave a hint of the trauma that lay ahead for them all.

Johnny had to undergo even more surgery after the pneumonia had cleared. That, too, was relatively successful, but he remained asleep – unconscious – and still in a deep coma. The Owens family remained hopeful throughout. If anyone could fight this, they reasoned, Johnny could. At the back of everyone's minds, as time went on, another much more painful scenario was taking the place of hope and optimism. It was hard not to allow darker thoughts to surface. They tried to think positively at all times and most days they succeeded.

In Mexico City, Lupe Pintor could find no solace. He had taken Johnny's situation very badly. Every day, he went to the old Catholic church in the La Colonia district of the city close to his home. It was the church he passed each morning on his training run, the church that often gave him inner peace. There he asked God for forgiveness and prayed that his comrade Johnny Owen would recover and survive. He questioned the devastation his hands had inflicted on another human being and was inconsolable. Lupe Pintor did not want to go on. He had lost the will to fight. The Owens family sent him a message of support and friends convinced him that he must return to his profession. Not just for his own state of mind, but for his future and those of his protégés. Mexican boxing needed Lupe Pintor. Without the support of Dick and Edith Owens and those close to him, Lupe Pintor would have thrown in his hand and quit the ring.

In Los Angeles, for those deeply and closely concerned with the welfare of Johnny Owen, events moved on swiftly. They seemed part dream, part reality. Time had no meaning. It seemed to either fly by or drag desperately depending on the kind of news they awaited or on their emotional mood. It was as though they were all part of some movie, some Monday night film for TV, or players in a story they had no control over. The sense of being stunned to a halt with shock as though they had walked into a wall seemed always to be with them. Dick, though, was firmly rooted in the camp of hope. He was certain his son would accompany him home to Wales one day soon. Others around the trainer were less optimistic.

Every Sunday throughout the vigil, the family went to the Welsh Presbyterian church just a few hundred yards away from where Johnny lay in hospital. As they sang at the chapel, they sang in hope. They sang and they prayed that the nightmare would soon be over. The chapel became their place. It was a place to reflect, to consider and to hope for better days to come. More poignant to the outside world was the unique show of unity and dignity the family and friends of the boxer displayed under almost continuous daily pressure during their visits to Johnny. The outside world, through the media, especially in the United Kingdom, were keeping their own kind of vigil. They were now taking a huge interest in the dramatic events slowly unfolding in the City of Angels. They were becoming part of their own story.

The newspapers at home were full of Johnny Owen. The tabloids carried a day-by-day progress report on the young man's condition. Experts were called upon to evaluate his chances. Debate over the dangers of boxing raged in the tabloids and broadsheets, on the TV and radio, and in public bars, watering holes and households all over the United Kingdom. Boxing was banned and resurrected daily. The clergy got stuck in, as did the politicians. Not many noted that the boxer as an icon usually hailed from a part of society that has little by way of wealth. Not many clergy, politicians and media spokespeople were quick to point out society's role in the outcome of the battle of Little Mexico. One didn't hear much about who was actually responsible for boxing. The big question – Why is boxing? – was rarely asked. All that most do-good pundits wished for was that boxing should be banned, legislated against and driven underground. The causes of boxing and the political requirements involved in the solution of boxing were rarely discussed.

On the ground, in the towns, villages, streets and houses, everyone talked of Johnny Owen, all of us. And all of us to a man, woman and child wanted him to win his last great battle because we knew in our heart of hearts that if he were to survive, he would surely never fight again – it would be his last great battle. We also knew that, if allowed to continue his life, he would once more in some way bring joy back into the hearts of the people who supported him so. That was Johnny's character after all. He always brought joy.

The media scrum was such that when the family visited their son the world did too. And what we all saw was always to concern us. What the family had to endure must have been even more upsetting. Their experiences would have been much more profound, more intimate and more disastrously soul-destroying. For what they saw daily, in that drab and feeble hospital bed, was the sight of Johnny Owen, that powerhouse of a fighter in the boxing ring, reduced to a still, hopelessly dependent young man. They kept their spirits up nonetheless.

They talked to him, laughed, joked and kidded with him and, when alone with him, they cried.

There were real scares, too. After one such scare, Johnny was declared clinically dead. But he fought back and rallied. It seemed that the fighter was giving it all he had and was defying the doctors and their pessimistic opinions whenever he could. For everyone concerned, what had started as a nightmare was now reality. Somehow, the human condition gets used to reality no matter how bad it becomes. Soon, that reality gives way to routine. Very often the only way to deal with anything truly traumatic is to find a routine. Make the life you have to lead during the trauma meaningful. Dick and Edith Owens followed the same routine almost every day. They would go to the hospital then walk around the complex and maybe downtown then return to the hotel. Everyone was kind to them – friends in Wales, friends in Los Angeles, police and medical staff, and friends who chose to stay close to them. The kindness shown often overwhelmed. It held them together and, despite being in a very unsafe neighbourhood and in a less-than-salubrious hotel, they felt comfortable. Each morning, Dick and Edith would get up, have breakfast, stay in their hotel room for a while and then visit the hospital. Then the next day it would start all over again. Routine has its bad points, no question of that, but in this case routine was their saviour.

Get-well cards, flowers, messages of goodwill and good wishes poured into the hospital. On 7 October 1980, the ex-heavyweight champion of the world, Muhammad Ali, was admitted to a ward close to where Johnny lay. Ali was suffering after his unsuccessful challenge to wrest the world crown from the great champion Larry Holmes. Muhammad, although very unwell himself, always asked how the Welshman was and often said a prayer for him, to aid his recovery and to wish him peace. The Secretary of State for Wales broke off a tour of trade and industry to visit Johnny. Disneyland offered Johnny's parents free rooms for as long as they needed them. A huge get-well card was sent from the people of Merthyr Tydfil. Back home, everyone in churches, chapels and beyond hoped and prayed Johnny would be all right. Business ran as usual at Johnny's grocery store. In pubs and clubs all over the South Wales valley area, funds were being collected to help the boxer and his family. The Mayor of Merthyr Tydfil sent sympathy wishes and the local Member of Parliament pledged his full support for the family.

On 13 October, it was reported that Johnny had been taken off the life-support machine. Although it was correct that Dr Holly had been pleased with Johnny's condition recently, there was no truth in the rumour that he had resumed normal breathing. His muscles had started to move more freely, but no one was getting through to him, there was no recognition. The respirator still kept him alive. Johnny's boxing manager, the still-distraught Dai Gardner, decided to go home to Wales 33 days after Johnny was first admitted into the hospital. He could do no more, was not feeling well within himself, and was considering his position and his future. He had declared openly that he might never manage another boxer again.

The weeks and days dragged on for those who remained. Spirits had to be kept up. Hope had to remain at the forefront of thinking. The vigil and the press interest continued. The routines hardened and became almost habit.

Thirteen days after Dai Gardner's departure, news came that brought a degree of hope. John Holly felt the coma might be lifting. His prognosis for the boxer was optimistic for the first time in weeks. This was promising news for Johnny's family. The next day would bring more hope and then the next might see Johnny awake. That's what they always believed. Those were the thoughts, no matter what. It was always possible Johnny would wake up out of the blue and say hello and ask what the fuss was about. Like all parents in this situation, Dick and Edith would not give up. They ruled out no scenario regardless of what anyone advised to the contrary. Johnny Owen was a fighter and he would be fighting. That was the reasoning that guided them. The prognosis for Johnny's immediate future seemed positive. Things suddenly looked brighter.

At approximately 7.30 p.m. that same evening, the telephone rang. Dick answered, to be told that Johnny was suffering from pneumonia and it seemed the doctors were not able to clear it up. Edith and Dick rushed over to the hospital. They were quickly ushered into Johnny's room. Johnny was struggling for every breath. The pneumonia was taking hold and it was clear that he was coming to the end of his short life.

When it came, it came peacefully. The room became silent. The silence was beautiful and calm, and those there sensed that all was well. It was 4 November 1980. Johnny Owen was dead. He was just 24 years old.

The morning after Johnny's death, Dick and Edith Owens began the work of arranging passage home for themselves and for their son. Funeral arrangements were quickly dealt with. Dick found the strength from somewhere to ensure everything was in place. The British Consulate fast-tracked all immigration red tape for them and new friends and old made sure they were well looked after as preparations to leave took hold. At home, the whole country seemed in mourning and the media watched every move.

Johnny Owen's life-and-death struggle had gripped the nation and emotionally involved almost everyone in the United Kingdom. It seemed to emulate and parallel the life-and-death struggle of us all and our industrial Welsh communities at that time, as factories threatened closure, and small towns and villages began to feel the effects of new policies aimed at massive economic and cultural change.

To witness our great sporting hero, our great Welsh hope, fallen and seemingly mortally wounded in a Los Angeles hospital, seemed, well, just a bit too much to bear for many of the country's browbeaten inhabitants. And when the unthinkable happened, we were dumbstruck. Hurt, in extreme disbelieving shock. What happened to 'our' Johnny on that awful, awesome night in Los Angeles burned deep.

Eddie Thomas, a famous boxing son of Merthyr Tydfil, summed it up perfectly when he talked of Johnny just after hearing the news of his death: 'You never think about it. It's never talked about. You never talk about people dying in the ring. It's like colliers going down the pit. You know it's dangerous but you do it just the same. Life is dangerous. If it isn't you're doing it wrong.' Even so, Eddie was in shock just like everyone else.

Dick and Edith soon flew back to the United Kingdom. After a little rest, and a solemn and respectful hotel press conference, they undertook what would be the gruelling three-hour journey to Merthyr Tydfil and home.

For Dick, the memory of leaving Merthyr Tydfil such a short time previously, to help take part in a boxing match in Los Angeles, would still have been burning brightly. It would have been in his mind, one can assume, all the way from London to Wales. He would have remembered the troop of cars and supporters that ushered them to Heathrow Airport, wishing them well on their way, just seven weeks previously. He would have remembered the hope and joy in all of their hearts as they travelled to America and to possible World Championship glory. He would have remembered his son, burning with ambition and happiness.

They arrived in Merthyr Tydfil exactly three hours after leaving London. It had seemed much longer on that damp, depressing day. Traffic along the M4 to Wales was its usual mess, cars bumper to bumper coming out of the capital eager to be on some journey or other to God knows where. The traffic thinned out soon after the Severn Bridge. Once across the water, they were home in Wales. Being home seemed real and right, but it seemed strange and more than a little unreal too. Johnny was not there to greet them.

The London Ex-Boxers paid tribute to Johnny Owen by awarding him the boxer of the year award for 1980. The Welsh Ex-Boxers made him boxer of the year, too. After all, Johnny had won the European title and defended his British title during that last year. His town and country remembered him and eventually honoured him. Then the final tribute took place in the High Street Chapel.

On a cold, rainswept November day, they carried the body of Johnny Owen from Merthyr Tydfil High Street Baptist Chapel to Pant Cemetery high above the town. Around 1,000 mourners and over 200 floral tributes gave testimony to how much Johnny was loved. They came from all over the globe to stand in silent vigil to the shy boxer they had named the Matchstick Man. There were wreaths and tributes from all kinds of people in all walks of life, one from Muhammad Ali and another from Tom Jones, and there were at least 1,000 mourners on the route from Merthyr town itself to the cemetery in Pant.

The Revd. Herbert Price spoke about Johnny at the funeral service and gave a moving eulogy, part of which read: 'Today, we mourn one of our folk heroes. A man of courage who took whatever life dealt out and took it unflinchingly. The measure of a man's life is not the number of years he has lived, but the way he has lived them. There are lads here in Merthyr Tydfil who are going to be better men because

Johnny Owen lived.'

20

MEETING LUPE PINTOR

In the autumn of 2002, ex-world bantamweight champion Lupe Pintor arrived in Merthyr Tydfil. On a damp, windswept, cold November day, he unveiled a statue to commemorate the life of Johnny Owen, his old gladiatorial adversary and one of the town's most famous sons. Dick and Edith Owens, Johnny's parents, thanked Lupe for his kindness in travelling all the way from Mexico City to Merthyr Tydfil to honour their son. He hugged them both. In honouring Johnny Owen, he was honouring himself as well.

The warm, spring, urban sunshine beamed bright and early that morning. I'd got up before anyone else had even dreamed about surfacing, breakfasted well, and decided to take a walk and relax a little. I wanted some time to come to terms with what I had experienced this past week, and what better time to consolidate one's thoughts than on the morning of the day of departure. It was Sunday, 11 March. We still had some work to do on the film, but basically it was time to pack up and head for home. Our flight was to leave Mexico City at 9 p.m. There were some 14 hours to go.

I approached the corner that led to the main road, where the traffic generally made life hell for everyone, and I smiled as I remembered Dick's and my reaction when first we saw all the cars and vans and trucks speeding up and down the crazy 16-lane inner-city highway. Today, it was almost quiet. Not serene or silent or empty or anything as ludicrous as that, just almost quiet. Astonishingly, I was able to cross this mad Mexican highway for the first time without fearing for my life. Cross without dodging, without giving up and returning to the safety of the pavement on the hotel side. It was a good feeling to walk almost nonchalantly across the road. It was a feeling of wresting one's power back, regaining freedom. I crossed to the other side, which meant I was in undiscovered territory – virgin pavements awaited Welsh footsteps. I knew that if I walked north from the point of crossing, I would eventually arrive at a park. A green oasis in the grey of the city. The park was called Jardin del Arte and was situated just off James Sullivan Avenue, no more than 200 metres from the hotel base. I'd seen it on the map pasted to the wall of the reception area at the hotel. I'd been trying to get there all week. Now I had a chance. So, north and to the Jardin it was.

The park was certainly green, which made a wonderful change from what I'd become used to. It wasn't green like Wales. Not at all. But it was rather splendid. And not huge, not by the standards of Hyde Park or Central Park, but still a welcome relief from the mad city and big enough to allow a good one-hour walk – circular, of course – around its perimeter. I bade a fond and genuine good morning to some of those out exercising and getting fit for the week ahead, for their lives ahead. Most replied in spirited and enthusiastic kind. And I began to wonder what the point of jogging was. What was it all about? To train and give the body hell day in day out, excessively and without purpose, seemed to me a little mad. If there is an attainable goal, a dream, an Olympic medal opportunity maybe or a career in boxing or team sports at the end of the punishment, then perhaps one could see the purpose and understand it. Still, each to his own. It is not for me.

I watched the joggers and the runners carefully. I thought of Johnny Owen, running up and down the hills and valleys of Wales. Johnny, when he was really fit, enjoyed life all right. I wondered if any of these fine folk enjoyed their lives or, I mused, were they merely keeping up appearances and perhaps fashioning an image with their daily fitness routine?

The day Dick Owens met Lupe Pintor had been a fascinating one. It began as all our days in Mexico City had begun, with a large and enjoyable communal breakfast. Breakfast had been the focal point, where we all met and plans for the day ahead were laid out, but on the morning of Dick's meeting with Lupe Pintor it did feel a little different. A nervous tension filled the air. From the filmmakers' point of view, it was a time for apprehension. The shots they wanted on film would have to come from one take and there would be little room for error or misjudgement. Yes, one or two of the moves had been scripted already. A little of the prospective action had been staged, but not much. One cannot, no matter how hard one tries, fake emotion or falsify the genuine. For the events we'd planned for late morning to work, it would have to go very smoothly indeed. Dick Owens too was a little subdued that breakfast time – for him, a long journey of almost half a lifetime was about to come to an end. He would have been collecting his thoughts and dealing with a very different set of emotions.

We'd arrived outside Lupe Pintor's home at around ten o'clock that morning. There, we camped for a while in our large white van, like some undercover cops from a cheap TV film, while a strategy was cobbled together in order to help us enact the forthcoming event – the meeting between Lupe Pintor and Dick Owens. The two men had never met. Not since we'd been in Mexico City. They hadn't even actually met in 1980 during the build-up to Johnny Owen's World Championship challenge either. At least not officially. They had probably bumped into each other on a daily basis, silently saluted each other from afar perhaps during that pre-fight time out there in foggy Los Angeles, but they hadn't really socialised or anything. They had a job to do back then and both were too busy doing that, one presumes. They were also in opposing camps. Fraternising with the enemy is not the done thing.

It was agreed that a camera would be quickly set up to film Dick's arrival at the house. He was to go to the top of the street, wait for a signal and then walk to Lupe Pintor's front gate, the muddy-green barrier that kept the world at bay from Lupe's private life. There, Dick would purposely wait. The camera would be repositioned and Dick would knock on the door. This was how it was supposed to work. How it had been planned. How it would be filmed. Hopefully, Lupe Pintor would then answer.

Nothing of the meeting itself had been choreographed or scripted. We all felt a sense of intrusion, and were well aware of the magnitude and importance of the events that had led to this encounter. We wanted to let it all happen without interfering too much. Those involved with the actual filming did their utmost to ensure the least possible hindrance to what was now to take place. Having said that, Dick understood perfectly that in order for the documentary to work, then certain obligations had to be met – one of which entailed the setting up of a pre-scripted shot or two. Earlier in the week, we'd agreed that some but not all of the filmed events would be worked out in advance and that the more important ones should be left to play out naturally. So what happened after Dick knocked on the gate would be anyone's guess. From there on in, nothing could be known. One by one, we all piled out of the van and, like something from a '70s TV series, we hit the streets.

Lupe Pintor's house was situated in the area he had been born into, the area that had given rise to his nickname, Cuajimalpa. It was a busy working-class part of the city. Lupe had stayed with his own kind and had presumably been suitably rewarded for his loyalty with a lifetime of local celebrity to help make his and his family's lot easier than the average Mexican's. It's good to have a world champion living down the road from you, to wave to and say hello to on the street, to pray next to at mass.

Lupe Pintor was also now training young men to box. And he was good at it. He had his own place, his own gym, situated deep in the heart of one of the poorer neighbourhoods in town. He had set himself up well. There, he gave something back to those who had given him so much opportunity and such support over the years of success and beyond. We'd gone to see him at the gym the day before his meeting with Dick. He had looked so at home with the youngsters, so at ease in passing on his trade. One could only wonder at the possibilities that might have lain ahead for Johnny Owen. Teaching is almost always good for the soul, especially if you have something unique in your experience to pass on and perhaps a star pupil to pass it on to. You learn in both your craft and in life, and you become really good at what you do; you become wise. Why waste that wisdom?

Lupe Pintor was clearly an excellent coach. He was happy with his life, with his teaching and his training. Here was a contented man. On that day at the gym at least, he was also clearly nervous and wanted to meet Dick Owens quite desperately it seemed. Resolving the tragedy of the past would help Pintor enormously. That much was clear.

Back at Lupe Pintor's house and across the way from where we were parked in our big white van, the fresh-fruit shops, newsagents and tobacconists were doing great business. Men, young and old, stood at the corner of the street in casual attire just chewing the fat, as men do on street corners and city benches all over the world. It's what they're supposed to do. There were seven of us: Dick Owens, Dylan, Ynyr, Huw, Raul our bodyguard, Jorge Eduardo Sanchez the translator, and me. The men chewing the fat glanced our way briefly. They checked us out and dismissed us with looks of disdain. Crazy people, they must have thought, pay them no heed. Dick Owens left the group and walked to a spot on top of a hill just around the corner from Lupe Pintor's house. The scripted scenario was played out successfully all the way to the word 'cut'. Dick then knocked. Slowly, the great green gate creaked open.

Lupe Pintor and Dick Owens looked first deep into each other's eyes. The look didn't last long – a second or two – but it was enough. It allowed them time to understand. Then the smiles came, and soon after the smiles came the hug. Almost 22 years had passed since the epic encounter between the Mexican champion and the son of the man he was now embracing. The powerful story of Johnny Owen and the Welshman's inimitable character had conspired to bring about their reunion. Tears flowed, from both sides. Dick Owens was quickly introduced to Lupe's family, his beautiful wife Victoria and their two sons. The serious business of filmmaking was completely forgotten in the emotion of the moment and everyone involved was caught up in the story. For Dick and Lupe, the camera was no longer there. Effortlessly, without thought for those around, but with the help of Jorge, the translator, they began to converse.

Dick forgave Lupe publicly, on tape, on the record, and absolutely absolved him from all blame for what had happened to his son. He told Lupe, for the first time, of Johnny's rare bone condition, something the ex-bantamweight champion could not, would not, have known about. Dick told the Mexican champion how no one had been aware Johnny had that kind of weakness, how if he or Johnny's family had known, then his son would never ever have boxed in the first place. Lupe responded emotionally and palpably with huge relief. These initial exchanges between the two men occurred almost spontaneously. It seemed that within minutes of their getting together, of sitting down in Lupe's comfortable living room, of trading hellos and quickly summarising the past 20 years or so, they talked of Johnny Owen and that last fight in Los Angeles. And as we, the film crew, outsiders each of us in this drama, looked on, the realisation that one thing above all was very evident began to surface. For both men, the idea of 22 years having passed since they last saw each other seemed nonsensical. To them, it seemed the fight had taken place yesterday, so fresh was the whole event in both of their minds. The two men talked away the rest of the day and talked boxing mainly.

Lupe Pintor was 48 years old in 2002. His home was typical middle-class Mexican Catholic. He tells all those who enter that his house is a house of love and that all invited therein are welcome. Lupe is hugely respected in Mexico these days. His world seems impregnable. Slowly, through Jorge Eduardo Sanchez, Dick Owens and Lupe Pintor began to get to know each other. Slowly, they became friends. Dick Owens eventually plucked up the courage to finally make the offer he had promised himself he was going to make to the ex-champion earlier in the week. He wanted Lupe Pintor and his wife Victoria to come to Merthyr Tydfil and unveil a statue in honour of Johnny Owen. Instinctively, without hesitation, Lupe Pintor agreed to the request. The two men shook hands on it. It was settled. In that handshake lay the bond. With this agreement in place, wheels could now be set in motion to make Dick Owens' dream of a statue in honour of his son a reality.

After a brief period of relaxation, film sets were hurriedly constructed out of rearranged furniture and ideas bandied about as to how best to use the house and surroundings to complete the day's work. I stepped outside, into the yard that the Pintors shared with two other houses, and kicked a loose football around, steering clear of the fierce dog tied to a wall close by. I figured the meeting between Dick and Lupe was over already, at least from the point of view of the outsider. They were clearly revelling in their conversation. The high emotion of the moment had passed, although everything they would discuss at this place and this time would always have Johnny Owen in its text, spoken or unspoken. Now they needed time to take it all in. Time to move on. Next would come the resolution. A private matter.

The next day – Thursday – we were all invited to a boxing match. Well, matches, actually, on a boxing bill. One of Lupe Pintor's star pupils was to fight. He was 'top of the bill'. It was no great Championship evening, just an academy of young boxers being put through their paces in front of a largely invited audience. Something the young Johnny Owen would have felt at home attending or even being a part of. You could see an up-and-coming Johnny Owen here maybe, or the next Lupe Pintor perhaps. A new generation of Mexican fighters was being shown to the world for the first time on television. The local TV station was to cover the show (by satellite) and we from Wales would be there to see it as special guests, at the invitation of Lupe Pintor. It was indeed a privilege to be there. It would be the first time Dick Owens had been near a boxing ring since 19 September 1980.

There were to be eight bouts on the bill that night. They would be fought hard and fast, and the entertainment value would be high, according to the pre-fight posters. When the television channel got wind of Dick Owens' attendance, they introduced him to the audience and to the viewers back home, half asleep, probably, in their armchairs, wondering what this man from Wales had to do with their evening's boxing. It was a proud moment for the old boxing trainer. The night passed by well. What must have been going through Dick's mind watching these young fighters and talking to their respective trainers? One can only hazard a guess. For the two days after our 'night at the fights', Dick became calm, subdued and very quiet, as we all did, come to think of it. When asked, he turned up for work like the good pro that he is, but mostly there was a kind of anticlimactic feel to the final few days in Mexico City. Which was hardly surprising. There was a lot to take in, a lot to think about. Minds were occupied.

I had finally completed the full circle around the circumference of the Jardin del Arte. Although a lot had been resolved for me and I had learned much of the story of Johnny Owen over the past week or so, I felt there was a lot more to try to understand before I could make my own sense of it all. There would be time for thought aplenty on the other side of the Atlantic back in cold, wet Wales. For now, it was time to return to the hotel and get on with this last day. There was still work to do and, before we were due to leave for the airport, a light, social meeting with Lupe Pintor and his family had been arranged in the Plaza de la Constitucion. We were to say our goodbyes there that afternoon.

The last day flew by. The meeting with Lupe, Victoria and their two children at the Plaza went well. A tearful farewell between Dick Owens and the ex-bantamweight world champion affected all present. They vowed to meet again when Johnny's statue was ready to be unveiled, Pintor promising faithfully he would attend the ceremony, come what may. Then he was gone.

There was time to visit the magnificent cathedral, and time to sit and reflect in quiet, personal prayer before one of the more resplendent altars, should one have wished to do so. We ticked off all of the remaining jobs with no real drama or any problems. Goodbyes all around were amicably extended to those that had been so kind to us at the hotel (including the hundreds of waiting staff) and to Jorge Eduardo Sanchez and Raul. Without their help, the week's successes could never have been achieved. We were at the airport and through Customs again before we knew it.

Looking down at the tarmac of Mexico City Airport for a final time, one could now only reflect on the week gone by. There was nothing to be done now. Nothing could be changed – the future was elsewhere. Mexico was the past now. In many ways, it had been a glorious time of bonhomie and fun. In many other ways, it had been a testing time – one not just to cast an eye on Johnny Owen's life and times, or Lupe Pintor's situation at home in Mexico City, but to consider all things, life itself: its delicacy and fragility.

We flew into the Mexican skies heading for Amsterdam and Europe. We waited for five hours for a connecting flight to Cardiff and Wales at Schiphol Airport. Then, outside Cardiff International Airport, we all shook hands and said our farewells, each going our separate ways home. The show was over. The fairground had packed up its kit and left town.

I was driven down the M4 in a taxi to my home in Carmarthen and my meagre writer's abode. It was getting dark and was very cold in comparison to the sunny spring weather we'd left behind in Central America. The talk in the cab was mundane and ordinary. It had been raining pretty much non-stop all week in Wales. There was a rugby match on Saturday – would Wales win? Someone from Llanelli said they'd heard a cuckoo. They must be bloody cuckoo. It's only March! Double rollover on the lottery this week! Have you seen the football results? On and on it went. I was so grateful for my companion. What a relief! There's Welsh life on earth, boyo!

It took about an hour and a quarter from the airport to home. I waved the cab driver farewell, opened the front door, stepped inside, kicking a pile of mail (bills mostly) to one side, and shut the world out.

WE'LL KEEP A WELCOME IN THE HILLSIDE

Far away a voice is calling,
Bells of memory chime,
Come home again, come home again,
They call through the oceans of time.

We'll keep a welcome in the hillside,
We'll keep a welcome in the glen,
This land you knew will still be singing
When you come home sweet home again.

There'll be a friendly voice to guide you,
On your return we'll always pray,
We'll kiss away each hour of longing
When you come home again some day.

We'll keep a welcome in the hillside,
We'll keep a welcome in the vale,
This land you knew will still be singing
When you come home again to Wales.

This land of song will keep a welcome,
And with a love that never fails,
We'll kiss away each hour of *hiraeth*
When you come home again to Wales.

POSTSCRIPT

Johnny Owen was, without question, one of the great heroes of Wales, one of the bravest soldiers of destiny this small country of ours will ever see. We (those of us associated with the documentary film that is) never had the opportunity of knowing Johnny personally but we came close enough to learn something of his character, close enough to taste the bitter flavour of unfair sadness. It was a pleasure to be a small part of the story of Johnny Owen. It was also undoubtedly an honour.

Ynyr Williams, producer of *Johnny Owen: The Long Journey*, March 2004

In December 2002, BBC Four the BBC's flagship documentary channel, showed for the first time *Johnny Owen: The Long Journey*. The 40-minute documentary featured Johnny Owen's father and ex-trainer, Dick Owens. It followed him on his journey from Merthyr Tydfil to Mexico City to meet Lupe Pintor, the ex-bantamweight boxing champion of the world. The two men had not met since the Los Angeles World Championship fight between Lupe Pintor and Johnny Owen on 19 September 1980.

The film won two Welsh BAFTA awards: one for best documentary drama of 2002, the other for Dylan Richards as best director. The programme was rated a huge success.

A year earlier, between 10 November and 9 December 2001, the play *Fighting Words* was performed to a packed audience at the Factory Theatre, Toronto, Canada. Its author, Sunil Kuruvilla, himself an ex-boxer, brought a novel boxing idea to the stage using Johnny Owen's last fight as a backdrop. On the front of the programme for that opening night were the words, 'A world premiere inspired by the true-life story of the Welsh boxing legend Johnny Owen'. The play was such a winner that it was commissioned to open in New York during the summer in 2004.

In the winter of 2002, Lupe Pintor arrived in Merthyr Tydfil. On a rainswept, cold November day, he unveiled a statue to commemorate the life of Johnny Owen, his old gladiatorial adversary. The statue now stands in Merthyr Tydfil's prestigious shopping centre. Johnny faces home and Gellideg.

There is much talk of a feature film concerning Johnny's life; more than one interested party is promoting the idea. His brother Kelvin runs an excellent website at www.johnnyowen.com. The story of Johnny Owen continues.

FOR THE RECORD

AMATEUR

Contests, 124: won 101, lost 23
Represented Wales 17 times, lost twice

1965	Finalist Welsh Schoolboys Championships
1970	Winner Welsh Schoolboys Championships
1971	Finalist Welsh Schoolboys Championships
1972	Finalist Welsh Junior Championships
1973	Winner Junior Championships
1973	Best Junior, Hoover ABC
1974	Finalist Welsh Senior Championships, four exhibitions

PROFESSIONAL

Contests, 28: won 25, lost 2, drew 1

Date	Opponent	Result		
30 Sept. 1976	George Sutton	W	PTS	8
9 Nov. 1976	Neil McLaughlin	D	PTS	8
23 Nov. 1976	Ian Murray	W	TKO	7
28 Jan. 1977	Neil McLaughlin	W	PTS	8
15 Feb. 1977	Neil McLaughlin	W	PTS	8
29 Mar. 1977	George Sutton	W	PTS	10
Welsh Bantamweight Title				
25 Apr. 1977	John Kellie	W	TKO	6
16 June 1977	Terry Hanna	W	TKO	4
21 Sept. 1977	George Sutton	W	PTS	8
29 Nov. 1977	Paddy Maguire	W	TKO	11
British Bantamweight Title				
23 Jan. 1978	Alan Oag	W	TKO	8
27 Feb. 1978	Antonio Medina	W	PTS	8
6 Apr. 1978	Wayne Evans	W	TKO	10
12 June 1978	Dave Smith	W	PTS	8
29 June 1978	Davy Lamour	W	TKO	7
25 Sept. 1978	Wally Angliss	W	TKO	3
2 Nov. 1978	Paul Ferreri	W	PTS	15
Commonwealth Bantamweight Title				
3 Mar. 1979	Juan Francisco Rodriguez	L	PTS	15
European Bantamweight Title				

19 Apr. 1979	Lee Graham	W	PTS	8
10 May 1979	Guy Caudron	W	PTS	10
13 June 1979	Dave Smith	W	TKO	12
17 Sept. 1979	Neil McLaughlin	W	PTS	10
4 Oct. 1979	Jose Martinez Garcia	W	TKO	5
29 Nov. 1979	Davey Vasquez	W	PTS	10
22 Jan. 1980	Glyn Davies	W	RTD	5
28 Feb. 1980	Juan Francisco Rodriguez	W	PTS	12

European Bantamweight Title

| 28 June 1980 | John Feeney | W | PTS | 15 |
| 19 Sept. 1980 | Guadalupe Pintor | L | KO | 12 |

WBC World Bantamweight Title

KEY

Win (W), Points (PTS), Technical Knockout (TKO), Retired (RTD), Lost (L), Knockout (KO), Draw (D)